In Those Days

In Those Days

Collected Writings on Arctic History

Book 3
Tales of Arctic Whaling

by KENN HARPER

INHABIT
MEDIA

Published by Inhabit Media Inc.
www.inhabitmedia.com

Inhabit Media Inc. (Iqaluit) P.O. Box 11125, Iqaluit, Nunavut, X0A 1H0
(Toronto) 191 Eglinton Avenue East, Suite 310, Toronto, Ontario, M4P 1K1

This project was made possible in part by the Government of Canada.

We acknowledge the support of the Canada Council for the Arts for our publishing
program.

Printed in Canada.

Library and Archives Canada Cataloguing in Publication

Harper, Kenn, 1945-, author
     Tales of Arctic whaling / by Kenn Harper.

(In those days : collected writings on Arctic history ; book 3)
ISBN 978-1-77227-179-9 (softcover)

     1. Whaling--Canada, Northern--History. 2. Whaling--Canada,
Northern--Anecdotes. 3. Whalers (Persons)--Canada, Northern--
Biography. 4. Canada, Northern--History--Anecdotes. I. Title.
II. Series: Harper, Kenn, 1945- . In those days ; bk. 3.

SH383.5.C3H37 2018   639.2'809719   C2018-901559-4

Table of Contents

Introduction   /1
A Note on Word Choice   /5
Preface   /7

Collected Writings
The Mythical Voyage of the *Octavius*   /11
William Scoresby Junior: Whaler Extraordinaire   /17
Fire from Ice   /20
Baffin Fair   /23
Encounters with Inuit   /28
The Disastrous Season of 1835   /31
The Loss of the *William Torr*   /36
The Landmark Rock at Durban Harbour   /40
Inuluapik and Penny Discover Cumberland Sound   /46
Over-Wintering: The First Winter in Cumberland Sound   /52
A Whaling Captain, a Discovery Ship, and the White House Desk   /56
The *Diana*, a Charnel House of Dead and Dying Men   /60
May Day on a Whaler   /66
Words from the Whalers   /70
Guests of the Whalers: Inuit in New England   /86
A Literary Icon in the Arctic: Arthur Conan Doyle   /97
The *Windward*: A Sturdy Arctic Ship   /103

James Mutch: An Arctic Whaleman   /111
George Comer: The White Shaman   /126
Saved by Inuit, Rescued by Whalers   /132
The Murrays of Peterhead: A Whaling Family   /139
The Dead Horse Song   /145
David Cardno: At Home in Cumberland Sound   /148
The Toll of the Arctic   /158
Captain George Cleveland: Whaler and Trader   /163
William Duval: Sivutiksaq of Cumberland Sound   /169
The Burning of the *Easonian*: The Last Whaler   /175
The Loss of the *Albert*   /179

Acknowledgements   /183

Introduction

This is the third volume to emanate from a series of weekly articles that I wrote over a ten-year period under the title Taissumani for the Northern newspaper *Nunatsiaq News*. This volume presents stories of whaling, most of them from the eastern Canadian Arctic and Davis Strait. They are stories of real events, many involving Inuit and *Qallunaat* (white people), and often the interactions between these two very different cultures. All of the episodes can be documented from the historical record. For some, there is an extensive paper trail; for others, it is scanty. Inuit maintain some of these stories as part of their vibrant oral histories. We need to know these stories for a better understanding of the North today, and the events that made it what it is. They enhance our understanding of Northern people and contribute to our evolving appreciation of our shared history.

I lived in the Arctic for fifty years. My career has been varied; I've been a teacher, businessman, consultant, and municipal affairs officer. I moved to the Arctic as a young man, and worked for many years in small communities in the Qikiqtaaluk (then Baffin) region— one village where I lived had a population of only thirty-four. I also lived for two years in Qaanaaq, a community of five hundred in the remotest part of northern Greenland. Wherever I went, and whatever the job, I immersed myself in Inuktitut, the language of Inuit.

In those wonderful days before television became a staple of Northern life, I visited the elders of the communities. I listened to their stories, talked with them, and heard their perspectives on a way of life that was quickly passing.

I was also a voracious reader on all subjects Northern, and learned the standard histories of the Arctic from the usual sources. But I also sought out the lesser-known books and articles that informed me about Northern people and their stories. In the process, I became an avid book collector and writer.

Most of the stories collected in this volume originally appeared in my column, Taissumani, in *Nunatsiaq News*. *Taissumani* means "long ago" in Inuktitut. In colloquial English it might be glossed as "in those days," which is the title of this series. The columns appeared online as well as in the print edition of the paper. So it did not come as a surprise to me to learn that I had an international readership. I know this because of the comments that readers sent me. I had initially thought of the columns as being stories for Northerners. No one was writing popular history for a Northern audience, be it indigenous or non-indigenous. I had decided that I would write history that would appeal to, and inform, Northern people. Because of where I have lived and learned, and my knowledge of Inuktitut, these stories would usually (but not always) be about the Inuit North. The fact that readers elsewhere in the world show an interest in these stories is not only personally gratifying to me, but should be satisfying to Northerners as well—the world is interested in the Arctic.

I began writing the series in January of 2005, and temporarily ended it in January of 2015. I recommenced it three years later. I wrote about events, people, or places that relate to Arctic history. Most of the stories—for that is what they are, and I am simply a story-teller—deal with Northern Canada, but some are set in Alaska, Greenland, or the European North. My definition of the Arctic is loose—it is meant to include, in most of the geographical scope of the articles, the areas where Inuit live, and so this includes the sub-Arctic. Sometimes I stray a little even from those boundaries. I don't like restrictions, and *Nunatsiaq News* gave me free rein to write about what I thought would interest its readers.

The stories are presented here substantially as they originally appeared in Taissumani, with the following cautions. Some stories that were presented in two or more parts in the original have been presented here as single stories. For some, the titles have been changed. There have been minimal changes and occasional corrections to text. I have occasionally changed punctuation in direct quotations, if changing it to a more modern and expected style results in greater clarity. A few stories are new—they have not yet appeared in *Nunatsiaq News*. These are included to fill gaps in the chronology or geographical scope of Northern whaling with a focus on Arctic Canada.

The chapters have been organized generally in chronological order. They are meant to be read independently.

Qujannamiik.
Kenn Harper
Ottawa, Canada

A Note on Word Choice

nuk is a singular noun. It means, in a general sense, "a person." In a specific sense, it also means one person of the group we know as Inuit, the people referred to historically as Eskimos. The plural form is *Inuit*.

A convention, which I follow, is developing that *Inuit* is the adjectival form, whether the modified noun is singular or plural; thus, an Inuit house, Inuit customs, an Inuit man, Inuit hunters.

The language spoken by Inuit in Canada is Inuktitut, although there are some regional variations to that designation. The dialect spoken in the western Kitikmeot region is Inuinnaqtun. That spoken in Labrador is called Inuktut.

The word *Eskimo* is not generally used today in Canada, although it is commonly used in Alaska. I use it if it is appropriate to do so in a historical context, and also in direct quotations. In these contexts, I also use the old (originally French) terms *Esquimau* (singular) and *Esquimaux* (plural).

In Those Days

I have generally used the historical spellings of Inuit names, sometimes because it is unclear what they are meant to be. The few exceptions are those where it is clear what an original misspelling was meant to convey, or where there are a large number of variant spellings.

Preface

The bowhead, or Greenland, whale drew Europeans into the Arctic in the early seventeenth century, first to the waters off Spitsbergen in the North Atlantic, and then inexorably west to the waters of the Greenland Sea, Davis Strait, and Baffin Bay. *Balaena mysticetus* it was called by scientists, and it was a leviathan, by far the largest animal in the Arctic, on land or sea. Reaching a maximum length of about sixty-five feet, it measured thirty feet around and could weigh in excess of sixty tons. Its tail flukes alone could measure over twenty feet from tip to tip. Its skin was dark black in colour, under the jaw it was pure white, and its belly was mottled with white.

To the Arctic whaleman, the length of the whale was secondary to the length of the baleen, a row of springy slabs hanging from the roof of the whale's gargantuan mouth, the dominant feature of the beast's massive head, which took up about one-third the length of its entire body. Baleen served to filter the whale's food, for this largest of Arctic animals fed on some of the sea's tiniest offerings—plankton. In whaler jargon, baleen was "whalebone," or often just "bone." Usually, instead of recording the length of the whale itself, a whaling logbook recorded the length of the largest slab of whalebone. Baleen was economically important. It was most well known for its use in fashion—corset stays and skirt hoops. But it also had many other uses where strength and flexibility mattered—in riding crops, whips, umbrella ribs, fishing rods, chair backs and bottoms, carriage springs, window blinds, and nets, to name but a few.

This magnificent whale also had the misfortune to yield large quantities of good-quality oil. Whale oil was used as both a lubricant and a source of light before the development of petroleum products and the advent of electricity. In the early nineteenth century, expanding cities and developing factories had insatiable needs for oil. And so the bowhead, to its own detriment, offered a double economic prize of both baleen and oil. One large whale could supply fifty barrels of oil and a ton of bone.

When whalers began to exploit the large stocks of bowhead in Davis Strait, they kept close to the Greenland coast and did not venture much north of Disco Bay. It was not until 1817 that two whalers, the *Larkins* and the *Elizabeth*, continued north along the Greenland coast, through the treacherous waters of Baffin Bay, and across to what is now the Canadian coast.

The next year, British explorer John Ross followed essentially the same route north and west in his unsuccessful search for the Northwest Passage through Lancaster Sound, then followed the east coast of Baffin Island southward before making for home. Basil Lubbock, chronicler of whaling in the Arctic, felt that Ross's unsuccessful voyage showed whalers the way to Baffin Island. He wrote, "This voyage of Captain Ross . . . showed that, after reaching the north and west waters, it was possible for them [the whalers] to work out of Davis Straits along the west land, with the probability of finding whales in all the numerous inlets and fiords on the way."

Shortly thereafter, a number of whaling vessels followed what was essentially Ross's route. It had the advantage that it avoided much of the ice that the whalers would have encountered had they been on the Baffin coast earlier in the season.

This route was, in fact, similar to that which their quarry, the bowhead, followed on its annual migration. These whales are thought to be a stock separate from that of the far North Atlantic, with wintering grounds among the broken pack ice northeast of Labrador, where Davis Strait meets the North Atlantic. Most of this stock moved north along the coast of west Greenland in April, May, and June, before crossing the "Middle Ice" of Baffin Bay, a treacherous, sometimes impassable mass of floating, drifting ice floes, and entering Lancaster Sound and other High Arctic bays and fjords in June. They fed as far north as Smith Sound and Jones Sound, and as far west as Barrow Strait and Prince Regent Inlet. In late August, they began their return south along the Baffin coast, although a small number returned along the Greenland coast. Other whales made their way through the Middle Ice to the east coast of Baffin Island or to Cumberland Sound. The whale population of Hudson Bay, the last to be exploited in eastern Canada, is thought to be a different stock of bowhead whales.

Whaling scholar W. Gillies Ross succinctly summed up the Davis Straight whaling routine as "a one-season counter-clockwise circuit of Davis Strait and Baffin Bay." It became the preferred route for almost all of the history of whaling off the coast of Baffin. It was modified, after 1840 and the rediscovery of Cumberland Sound, to include that body of water in the itinerary of vessels that were not full before reaching the vicinity of Cape Dyer. Later, many vessels would head directly to Cumberland Sound and, after 1860, to Hudson Bay.

The vignettes that follow on whaling history deal almost exclusively with whaling in Canadian waters of the eastern Arctic, a trade that was dominated by Scottish and American whalers.

The Mythical Voyage of the *Octavius*

In 2011, an article appearing in a Canadian newspaper began with the bold assertion that Roald Amundsen, the first man to successfully navigate the Northwest Passage, was not really the first, but that he had been beaten by an unknown captain 143 years earlier.

The article then launched into an account of the incredible voyage of the *Octavius*. I had long known the story of this phantom ship, but I had never expected to see this fabulous fiction passed off as unassailable fact. Here is the story.

On August 12, 1775, the *Herald*, an American ship, was whaling in ice-choked waters west of Greenland. It was an unproductive day. Eventually the lookout in the crow's nest spotted another ship at some distance, slowly making her way toward the *Herald*.

In Those Days

As it neared, the crew realized that the mysterious ship was simply drifting their way with the current, her sails in tatters and her masts caked with ice. Captain Warren did not recognize the ship but hailed her nonetheless. There was no response.

Warren took a whaling boat crewed by eight men to the strange vessel and drew alongside. But still, there was no sign of life. Before going aboard, he discerned the name *Octavius* on the ice-battered hull. Accompanied by four sailors, Warren cautiously boarded the ship. They saw no one. Descending into the crew quarters, they saw a horrifying sight. Twenty-eight crew members were wrapped in blankets in their bunks. In the captain's cabin, they found the captain dead at his desk, his pen beside him. A woman's body was found frozen solid in his bed. A frozen sailor sat cross-legged on the cabin floor. Holding a flint and steel in his hands, he had evidently been trying to strike a fire—there was a small pile of wood shavings in front of him.

Captain Warren retrieved the logbook from the captain's cabin. As he studied it, his incredulity grew. The last entry had been made over twelve years earlier, on November 11, 1762! On that day the ship had been beset by ice for seventeen days. But what strained the captain's belief even further was the last position recorded in that logbook—160° west longitude, 75° north latitude. That position was north of Point Barrow, Alaska. There was only one conclusion that Captain Warren could draw—that the *Octavius* had drifted for over a decade, with the ice and currents of the Arctic Ocean, into and through the Northwest Passage, until she came out into Baffin Bay and continued her aimless drift through the ice-choked waters of Davis Strait.

The *Octavius* had left England for Asia in 1761 and reached its destination the following year. For some reason, the captain decided to return to England through the Northwest Passage, which had never been traversed but which allegedly lay north of North America. He became trapped in the ice, and his ship, with a crew of dead men, had conquered the Northwest Passage.

And that's where the recent report conveniently ended. But there is more.

Of course, the ship was never seen again after it left the sight of Captain Warren of the *Herald*. And its logbook, conveniently, has never surfaced either, and so has never been subject to scrutiny. In fact, it seems the origin of this entire story is recent. It first turns up in a book by Vincent Gaddis called *Invisible Horizons: True Mysteries of the Sea*, published in 1965. Gaddis provides no sources. And he was not free from controversy himself—he was the man who coined the sensational term *Bermuda Triangle* in a 1964 article for *Argosy* magazine. Gaddis was not averse to taking an item—true or not—and embellishing it into a mystery.

The *Octavius* has taken its dubious place in maritime lore alongside other phantom ships. But the ghost of Roald Amundsen need not fear for the posthumous removal of his claim as first to navigate the Northwest Passage. The *Octavius* is a myth. And shame on the reporter who resurrected this unfounded tale and tried to pass it off as fact.

But what is the source of the myth?

* * *

While perusing some books on Arctic whaling, I came across a whaler's tale that bears a striking similarity to the *Octavius* story. The name of the ship is different, and there is no reference to the mystery vessel having traversed the Northwest Passage. But the date of the alleged entry in the logbook of the ghost vessel is exactly the same—November 11, 1762.

The story was originally told by John Warrens, captain of a British vessel, the *Try Again*. Here is the story as recounted by Basil Lubbock in *The Arctic Whalers* in 1937:

> [In August 1775, the *Try Again*] was fishing at the edge of the ice in 77 degrees North. After a night of wind and snow and continual danger from pancake ice she found herself in a lead between two floes. The wind had died down to a cheerful northerly breeze before which the ship was headed in order to get clear and avoid being beset.
>
> As the *Try Again* came round a bend in the lead she sighted a brig about 2 miles away standing down the channel ahead of her. The presence of this vessel puzzled the captain, for only the day before there was not a ship to be seen from his crow's nest, and Captain Warrens reckoned that the brig must have been beset in the midst of the pack. It was soon noticed that the brig was not sailing and, as the *Try Again* overhauled her, it was perceived that there was no one at her helm for she kept coming up in the wind and then falling off, and sometimes even cannoned off the ice from one side to the other of the lead. Soon the state of her rigging could be seen. Her yards were swinging about anyhow with the braces trailing and only the bolt rope and a few tatters along the yards remained of any of her sails.
>
> As the *Try Again* came up to her the brig drifted aground on a low point of the ice. Captain Warrens immediately called away his boat's crew and rowed off to her. The brig was evidently a derelict but the superstitious Greenlandmen

[whalers] could hardly believe that she was real. . . . Only the stoutest-hearted manned the captain's boat. As the derelict was approached it became evident that she had been adrift for a long time. An ice-line cut deep into her timbers and her hull was scarred and gashed by old ice wounds. Frozen snow lined her yards, her tops and her rails.

The boat rowed up from astern and her name, *Gloriana*, could still be read though some of the letters were hardly decipherable. As the whale-boat drew alongside, the captain stood up and looked in through the stern windows. Seated in a chair at the head of the saloon table was a man apparently studying a chart. Captain Warrens thereupon hailed the ship in stentorian tones, *"Gloriana*, ahoy!"* But there was no movement or answer from the man in the cabin.

The boat's crew then clambered on deck and prised open the hatchway, which was covered deep in frozen snow. As the captain led the way down the cabin companion, a horrible dank mildewed smell came up. For a moment horror gripped the exploring boat's crew, but mastering their feelings they flung open the cabin door and peered in. The man whose back only had been seen through the window now faced them. They were looking at a corpse, whose open staring eye-balls and sunken cheeks were horribly filmed by a green mould. A quill was frozen to the fingers of the dead man's hand, and upon the chart lay an open logbook. Captain Warrens bent over and read the last entry: "November 11, 1762—We have now been 17 days in the ice. The fire went out yesterday, and our master has been trying ever since to kindle it again without success. His wife died this…" The sentence was unfinished.

In another cabin the body of a woman was found lying in the bunk, whilst crouching down beside the small cabin stove was the dead captain with flint, steel and tinder actually beside him. In the fo'c'sle lay the crew dead in their blankets. Of fuel and provisions there were none.

Seizing the logbook Captain Warrens returned in sudden panic to his own ship from the tragic brig and hurriedly crowded sail towards the open sea, fearful lest his ship should be beset and his fate be like that of the *Gloriana*'s crew.[1]

Lubbock thought that this yarn didn't ring true, but thought that it was, nonetheless, illustrative of the fate of many missing whaling crews.

The fact that the date in the alleged logbook in this tall tale is exactly the same as the logbook date in Vincent Gaddis's 1965 book, combined with the almost identical name of the captain, the identical number of days in the ice, the reference to flint, steel, and tinder, and the presence of the captain's wife on board, would seem sufficient to pinpoint this whalers' yarn as the source of the *Octavius* myth.

---

[1] Basil Lubbock, *The Arctic Whalers* (Glasgow: Brown, Son & Ferguson, 1937), 38–39.

William Scoresby Junior

Whaler Extraordinaire

A scientist who met William Scoresby Junior when the latter was fifty-two years of age described him succinctly as "eminent for qualities seldom united in one man." That scientist, James Joule, went on to describe Scoresby more fully in these words: "At once an experienced seaman, a successful geographical discoverer, a hardworking and eloquent clergyman, he was also a zealous student of nature and a scientific investigator."

William Scoresby Junior, born in 1789, was for twelve years the most successful captain and the most skilled navigator in the entire Greenland whaling fleet. Others followed where he led. Born in 1789 near Whitby, England, he went regularly to the whale fishery with his father from the age of ten, attended the University of Edinburgh for two winters while in his teens (studying natural philosophy and chemistry), was first mate under his father at the age of seventeen, and became captain in his own right at twenty-two.

While whaling was his reason for being in the Arctic, he used the opportunities his profession afforded him to study geology, meteorology, glaciology, terrestrial magnetism, and natural history.

Scoresby's correspondence with Sir Joseph Banks, president of the Royal Society, during the winter of 1817–18 helped to rekindle the British government's interest in the Northwest Passage and influenced the decision to send out the expedition of 1818 in search of the passage.

And our first real knowledge of the east coast of Greenland comes from Scoresby, who, in 1822, surveyed and mapped four hundred miles of that coast. One of the two main modern communities on that coast, the artificially created Scoresbysund, was named in his honour on its establishment by Ejnar Mikkelsen in 1925. (It is now known by its Greenlandic name of Ittoqqortoormiit.)

In addition to all his scientific accomplishments, coupled with his career as a successful whaler, Scoresby was a prolific writer. A member of the British Association for the Advancement of Science, Scoresby authored over sixty scientific papers. At the age of thirty-one, he wrote a popular Northern classic, *Account of the Arctic Regions and Description of the Northern Whale Fishery*, and three years later, in 1823, followed it with *Journal of a Voyage to the Northern Whale Fishery*.

That same year, following the death of his wife, he gave up his life at sea to become a clergyman in England, and served a number of parishes. The next year he was elected a Fellow of the Royal Society. In 1827, he was made an honorary member of the Paris Academy of Science. In 1839, he earned the degree of doctor of divinity.

Few men have amassed as great a knowledge of the physical and natural sciences in the Arctic in so short a time, or shared it so eloquently, as did William Scoresby.

To his many other accomplishments can be added the role of inventor. He developed an instrument that he called the marine diver, a tool for obtaining deep-sea temperatures. Using it, he established that in the Arctic seas the bottom temperatures are warmer than those of the surface.

Always curious, even in retirement, at the age of sixty-seven William Scoresby made one last major journey. He travelled to Australia to obtain data for his theories on magnetism. In the following year, 1857, he died at his home in Torquay, England, after a lifetime of diverse accomplishments.

Fire from Ice

William Scoresby was fascinated by ice, by its beauties, its composition, and its dangers. "Of the inanimate productions of the Polar Seas," he wrote, "none perhaps excite so much interest and astonishment in a stranger as the ice in its great abundance and variety."

Scoresby was not the first to observe that the ice that sailors called "fresh-water ice" could concentrate the rays of the sun in the same way as a convex lens of glass can, to produce heat and eventually fire. This fresh-water ice of the sailors was not what we consider freshwater ice today; rather, it was the ice from fields, ice floes, and icebergs. The small pieces used to create fire, he said, were distinguished by their black appearance when floating in the sea; they were transparent when removed from the sea and taken into the air. This ice was fragile but hard; the edges of a broken piece could cut like glass.

Scoresby wrote of how he often astonished the sailors on his ships by lighting their pipes using nothing but a piece of this transparent ice. "With a lump of ice, of by no means regular convexity, I have frequently burned wood, fired gunpowder, melted lead, and lit the sailors' pipes, to their great astonishment, all of whom . . . eagerly flocked round me, for the satisfaction of smoking a pipe ignited by such extraordinary means."

In forming the lens for this apparent magical feat, Scoresby roughed it out with a small axe, next scraping it with a knife, and finally polishing it with nothing but the warmth from his hand. He would hold the lens, once formed, in a gloved hand to perform the lighting. The sailors were equally impressed by the fact that the ice remained firm, although the rays emanating from it were hot enough that they would burn an exposed hand in a few seconds.

The experiment of creating fire from ice was first recorded by a European doctor, John Daniel Major, in 1671. Scoresby, a voracious reader, may have read about Major's accomplishment. But he may just as easily have discovered it himself through his innate curiosity about everything to do with ice.

In 1864, Jules Verne, the originator of modern science fiction writing, appropriated Scoresby's methods in *The Desert of Ice*. Captain Hatteras, in an attempt to reach the North Pole, had been abandoned with a few loyal men by mutinous crew members. Hatteras had wood for a fire but no means to ignite it. The ship's doctor hit upon an idea and explained, "We want to make the sun's rays converge to a common focus, and ice will do as much good as crystal."

As Scoresby had prescribed, the doctor first found a piece of fresh-water ice. From there, the description follows Scoresby's method exactly: "He began to smooth it with a hatchet; then he equalized the surface still further with his knife; then he polished it with his hand, and he obtained soon a lens as transparent as if it had been made of the most magnificent crystal. . . . The sun was shining brightly; the doctor held the lens so that the rays could be focused on the tinder, which took fire in a few seconds."

Like Scoresby's sailors, the doctor's companions were astonished.

Inuit, apparently, never discovered this ingenious method of creating fire. It is known, however, that they discovered what may be considered its opposite. Some Inuit used a concave piece of ice as a window in a winter or spring snow house, to diffuse light and spread it more broadly to light more of the interior of the domicile.

Baffin Fair

Davis Strait and Baffin Bay were dangerous bodies of water, and whaling was an occupation fraught with hazards. The reckless pursuit of profits resulted in ten ships lost in Baffin Bay in 1819. But that was only the beginning. During the 1830s, the British whaling industry in the Arctic suffered a series of disasters that threatened to destroy the industry completely.

In 1830, ninety-one British ships entered the unusually fierce weather of Davis Strait unprepared. Many did not return, and most of those that did were badly damaged, with a very poor catch to show for their trouble. A number returned to their ports "clean," whaler parlance for "empty," and almost every surviving ship had been damaged.

The fleet had sailed easily through open water up the west coast of Greenland. By June 10, almost a month earlier than usual, fifty vessels were near the Devil's Thumb, a landmark column of rock on the coast of Melville Bay, awaiting an opening in the ice through which to make a crossing to the Baffin coast. It was whaling custom that the sailors would doff their hats and salute this impressive landmark when passing it. When the ice finally opened, twenty-three ships headed into the water, with more following. The ice closed behind the leaders, separating this advance portion of the fleet into two groups of ships. Another group of ships, farther south, was also beset by ice.

The ice was heavy. When a storm arose on June 23, the whalers knew they were in trouble. By the following night, the wind had reached gale force. Hail and snow added to the dangers. Nine ships were lost that night. Others were saved only by being lifted by the pressure of the ice onto the pack itself. Two days later, the middle fleet felt the brunt of the storm, and another ship, the *William and Ann*, was wrecked. On June 30, the most southerly ships were hit by a gale, and a number of other vessels were destroyed.

The *Achilles* was lost on June 24. Alexander Kidd left an account of how survivors were brought home aboard ships that survived:

The crews of the *Achilles* and the French ship were taken on board of the *St. Andrew* of Aberdeen, and kindly treated. The number of hands on board of the *St. Andrew* now amounted to one hundred and fifty, and as the provisions were insufficient for so many, the majority of the shipwrecked crews resolved to proceed to some vessels which were perceived about twelve miles distant. Provisions were served out to them, and what clothes they had saved were put into the boats, which were dragged along the ice. The journey occupied about sixteen or seventeen days, during which the seamen were subjected to great privations by the inclemency of the weather, and some of the boats were destroyed which contained the few articles they had previously

saved. On the 13th or 14th of July, they reached their destination, and were kindly and hospitably received by Captain
Stevenson, of the *Horn*. There were at one time nine boats'
crews on board of that vessel, but a number of them were
afterwards transferred to others.[1]

In July, more ships were beset and more wrecked. It was not
until late August that leads began to open and some ships managed to reach the "West Land"—Baffin Island. But it was too late
in the season for serious whaling.

A captain whose name has not survived, of a ship that is unfortunately also nameless, wrote a touching description of watching
his ship succumb to the ice:

> On the 2nd of July our vessel, along with four others, was
> caught by the ice, which came with such overwhelming
> force against her, that it fairly lifted her out of the water,
> on the surface of the ice, as if to give us the last look of her,
> before she parted. She made a most majestic appearance,
> standing as upright as if she had been docked. It was not be-
> fore the water had reached the cabin sole that I abandoned
> her, to take my seat on my chest that was standing on the
> ice, there to witness the last struggle of our gallant bark.
>
> I am unable to depict the magnificent scene that pre-
> sented itself to my view; but it is one which would have suited
> either poet or painter. The first symptoms of destruction

---

[1] Alexander Kidd, quoted in Arthur C. Credland (ed.), *Baffin Fair: Experiences of George Laing, a Scottish Surgeon in the Arctic Whaling Fleet, 1830 and 1831* (Beverley, East Yorkshire, England: Hutton Press, 2003), 31.

appeared among the half-deck planks; then the standing rigging and stays became slackened and nothing was heard but the crashing of the hull as she went to pieces. Her masts meantime slowly bent toward each other, as if to take their final adieu; and when they came in collision, they seemed to say, "and must we part?" They then fell with a tremendous crash, and the hull was buried forever beneath a floe of ice six feet in thickness.[2]

In all, nineteen ships were wrecked, and twelve seriously damaged. More were beset by the ice for lengthy periods of time. Chaos ensued. A thousand or more men were camped on the ice of Baffin Bay. According to whaling custom, the shipboard discipline ended with the wreck of a vessel; these men, then, were free and not bound to obey their officers. The ensuing free-for-all became known in whaling lore as Baffin Fair. It was a custom among Arctic whalers—"an old and very stupid custom," in the words of whaling historian Basil Lubbock—to set fire to wrecked ships once everything easily salvageable had been taken from them. They burned them to the water line, allowing chests and casks from the hold to float free. In the first week of July, flames and smoke were seen over a vast expanse of Baffin Bay. Rum casks had been saved from many of the vessels, and the men helped themselves liberally to the contents. They ran about, played games, and tried to ignore the dangerous situation in which they found themselves. Miraculously, no lives were lost as a direct result of the shipwrecks. However, a number of drunken sailors died of exposure after wandering away from their camps on the ice.

---

[2] Anonymous, quoted in Credland, *Baffin Fair*, 30–31.

When word of the disasters in Baffin Bay reached English and Scottish ports, the price of whale oil rose quickly to £60 a ton. Twenty-one ships returned home clean. In 1830, the British fleet incurred total losses of £142,600 and recorded returns of a meagre £55,265. That year, Basil Lubbock wrote, was the "worst year in the whole history of Arctic whaling," and the bacchanalian excesses of Baffin Fair would long be remembered among whalers.

Encounters with Inuit

Whalers encountered Inuit on the Baffin coast, as they had much earlier on the Greenland coast. They made generally friendly contact and traded with them. Probably these contacts began early in the 1820s, but surviving accounts by whalemen are few. One of the earliest we have was written by John Wanless, surgeon—although only seventeen years old— aboard the *Thomas* of Dundee, who met Inuit from Pond Inlet on July 7 and 8, 1834.

The common term for Inuit at the time was *Esquimaux*, but Wanless used instead the more modern spelling *Eskimo*. However, he used this only once in his journal, instead usually referring to the people as *Yacks*, a term that Scottish whalemen generally used for Inuit.

Wanless described his first encounter with Inuit on the Baffin coast:

Monday 7 July. At 4 A.M. . . . two sledges with Eskimo were seen coming to the ship. They came on board and a terrible noise was made endeavouring to imitate the words said by the men. The two women or cunas were dressed in watery poops with a long pendant fore and aft, short trousers, and large boots wide enough to contain a child. The poop is supplied with a hood into which one of them had a young infant. They were tattooed upon the brow, cheeks, chin and thighs, by what I could not learn. They nor the men would taste not spirits. I gave all my needles nearly to them and some thread, as these seemed to be very much thought of. They had not anything to give in return. I fired a gun and all of them ran and put their hands on their ears, very much surprised.

They all departed from us—four pikininies, three men and two women—and went along the ice to another ship to the southward of us. They were greatly astonished at looking in a mirror and, observing the contrast, started back holding up their hands.[1]

The young surgeon continued his description of the Inuit clothing and appearance:

"Seals' skins principally afford their clothes but they have deer skins and bears', sewed with tendons. Their cheek bones are high and are far separated, hair long and dark hanging over their shoulders; black eyes and sharp; skin of a tawny colour. Hands and feet are exceedingly small in proportion to their body."

---

[1] John Wanless, quoted in W. Gillies Ross, *Arctic Whalers, Icy Seas* (Toronto: Irwin Publishing, 1985), 66.

In Those Days

The following day, they were visited by a different group of Inuit:

At six, four sledges of Yacks came to us, different from the former. They stayed on board two or three hours. I went along the floe about a quarter of a mile with them, giving buttons all the time to keep the peace. I offered a good deal of things for a young dog they had. It seemed to be a great favourite of the cuna belonging to the sledge and for this reason I imagine Yack himself was prevented from making the bargain. Fifteen to twenty dogs in a sledge. One of them had a unicorn's horn made into a lance. I procured it. We had all of them in the cabin eating fat.[2]

Wanless's account is probably representative of early encounters and trade between whalemen and Inuit along the Baffin coast.

Inuit benefited from the presence of whalemen in ways other than through direct trade. They were able to salvage meat from the flensed carcasses of whales or from whales that were struck but not captured and subsequently died and washed up onshore. These carcasses attracted bears and foxes, which the Inuit also used as food. They were also able to salvage wood and iron from the wrecks of ships along the coast.

---

[2] Wanless, quoted in Ross, *Arctic Whalers, Icy Seas,* 66.

The Disastrous
Season of 1835

Although the counter-clockwise circuit of Davis Strait and Baffin Bay was the preferred route for whalers to reach the Baffin coast, there were variations necessitated by weather and ice. In years when it was impossible to reach Baffin Bay by travelling up the Greenland coast, ships would try to cross to the west, south of the Middle Ice, that barrier of moving ice that often prevented passage north. Often, they would use the high cliffs of Cape Searle, north of Cape Dyer, as a landmark, and fish off the east coast of Baffin. Home Bay and Merchants Bay were particularly productive whaling grounds.

Stubbornly, those companies that had survived the financial disaster of 1830 returned their ships, just as unprepared, to Davis Strait. Owners continued generally to provision their ships for a summer season only, with no allowance for emergency supplies.

In Those Days

The year 1835 was as memorable as had been the year of Baffin Fair, and this time the disaster was even closer to Baffin. Only six ships were lost, but eleven were trapped by ice near Home Bay, midway down the Baffin coast, and six hundred men were forced to winter in the Arctic with scanty provisions. The loss of life was much more severe this time. About 135 whalers died of frostbite and scurvy that winter. To top it off, the fishing was poor. By the end of November, two of the trapped ships had been wrecked, and four had escaped the ice and made for home. Five remained trapped in the cold and increasing darkness of Davis Strait, drifting inexorably southward with the pack.

The *Viewforth* left Kirkcaldy, Scotland, on April 2 with a crew of fifty men. Keeping to the eastern shores of Davis Strait, she made her way north but was unable to break through the ice to reach a favourable location for whaling. She retraced her course partway down the Greenland coast, then crossed the strait to the Baffin coast. On June 30, she, along with the *Jane* from Hull and the *Middleton* from Aberdeen, was beset there and remained in the grip of the ice, drifting steadily southward, until January 30.

An anonymous crew member later recorded his memories of the ordeal. Shortage of provisions and scurvy were very much in his thoughts. On October 1: "My mind is made up for a winter in the Arctic Regions. The worst of it is, all the ships are very short of provisions; we are now on one and a half biscuits a day, one half pound of beef, and about half a teacupful of meal." By December 12: "I feel I am really starving." On January 8: "Many of our men are complaining, mostly of scurvy, and some of them are delirious." Three days later: "Six of our stoutest men are at present laid up, and can scarcely move a limb. Whenever they get any help to crawl out of bed, they swoon away. Their gums are hanging down separate from their teeth." In mid-January: "Three pounds of bread per week—about a biscuit a day. I am falling away to a shadow, through cold, and hunger, and thought."

And yet, in such desperate and threatening circumstances, one crew member was able to find beauty:

> I have just come off the deck, after enjoying a walk contemplating the moon-lit scenery. The evening is most beautiful; not a cloud, or speck, is to be seen in the serene sky. It is beyond the power of mortal man to conceive the scene that now surrounds us—the very land seems sunk in repose, and appears to rest more heavily on its foundations. Let a person conceive himself standing in the centre of an immense plain—let him look around him as far as the eye can penetrate, and he sees it filled with innumerable hills and hillocks of ice, whiter than marble, and of the most grotesque shapes imaginable. Such is our situation.[1]

William Elder, an officer of the *Viewforth*, published a memoir of his experiences crowded aboard ship with seventy other men, many of them refugees from ships that had already gone down. On December 10, he wrote:

> This morning at four o'clock it blew very hard with a blinding sleet, the ice roaring and crashing in an awful manner. It would be indeed a difficult thing for the human imagination

---

[1] Anonymous, *Sufferings of the Ice-Bound Whalers* (Allerthorpe, York, England: K Book Editions, n.d.), 21 (originally published Edinburgh: William White and Co., 1836).

In Those Days

to conceive the sensations produced upon our minds by our solitary ship drifting and working her way through regions of eternal frosts. Whole fields of ice as far as the eye can reach, along a coast which presents nothing but desolation in one of its most awful forms, frowning cliffs behind which are glaciers as far as the eye can penetrate—no home there for us if we were happening to lose our ship. Within fifty paces all around us the ice has squeezed as high as our ship and still the goodness of providence has delivered us. I may say with all safety that certain destuction was within fifty paces of us....

I have just now left the twixt-decks where I saw a more shocking sight. The poor lad that got his feet frozen is in a bad state. His feet are falling away by the ankles. They are rotting off; the smell they have is dreadful. Gangrene has commenced its direful operations, and the surgeons are afraid of his life. Scurvy has not spread any more amongst us yet, which is very pleasing for us. We have only the three cases yet and little appearance of them getting any better. We had service tonight.[2]

Yet amid it all, Elder, too, managed to occasionally find beauty. In late November, off the Baffin coast in the vicinity of Cape Dyer, he wrote, "The land that we were driving past now is awfully romantic, which consists of nothing but tremendous mountains which present to the eye a thousand fantastic forms such as the appearance of ruined castles &c." And later, "This has turned

---

[2] William Elder, quoted in Ross, *Arctic Whalers, Icy Seas*, 80.

out a most beautiful evening, not a cloud in the sky nor a breath of wind. Everything seems to be at rest. The moon is on the wane now too. It is really a night for contemplation. Eternity is in these moments."

After a drift of about six hundred miles, the *Viewforth* finally broke free of the pack in the North Atlantic off the coast of Labrador at the end of January. She reached Stromness fourteen days later carrying fourteen corpses, and with only seven men capable of manning the vessel.

The Loss of the *William Torr*

The year 1835 was a disastrous one in the Davis Strait whale fishery. Six ships were lost. A number of others were frozen in and forced to spend an unexpected winter in the Arctic. The *Jane*, the *Middleton*, and the *Viewforth* were all beset by ice within sight of the Baffin Island shore. Another, the *William Torr*, under Captain Smith, was frozen in farther north. Eventually most of the ships were accounted for—they were either reported as sunk or straggled into ports in Shetland or Orkney. The only one not heard from was the *William Torr*.

Many years later, a Shetlander who was a crew member of another ship described the last sighting of the ill-fated *William Torr*:

> I was still but a boy. I shipped at Lerwick on board the *Harmony* of Hull in the early spring of that year, and we sailed for Davis' Straits. The whale season was a bad one, and towards the end of August or the beginning of September we tried to get back to the east side of Baffin's Bay, and so, by coming down along the Danish settlements, to get home again.

The ice was very bad to get through—loose and thick all round, so that we had to shove her through every yard of the way. On the 11th of September there were three ships of us in company: the *William Torr*, the *Swan,* and ourselves. We were keeping together, as we were all working in the same direction, and we didn't well know what might happen any minute to some one or other—so it was good to keep within hailing distance if possible. Well, as night was coming down . . . we were just alongside the *William Torr*—both ships shoving through among the loose ice—when her captain hailed ours, and recommended him to bring up alongside a great curving mass of ice which lay quite close to both ships.

But our old man, not liking the looks of it . . . determined to push on a bit farther. The *William Torr*, however, hauled up to the ice and brought-to for the night. . . . We ran on for about an hour, and by that time came up with a very solid looking floe of ice, which, having a good bight in it, offered a sort of harbour. . . . We made all snug for the night and brought up there. By midnight, the ice was closing all around, and at two o'clock in the morning we were hard and fast. From the mast-head at daybreak, nothing but ice could be seen, with the masts of the *Swan* in the distance, and still farther off . . . we saw the mast-heads of the *William Torr*. But that was the last sight of her by mortal man, for next day she was gone; and we knew then that our master was right, and that she had been made fast to a loose floe, and that the under current had taken her off.[1]

---

[1] Anonymous, "Frozen In," *Once a Week* (January 3, 1863): 39.

In Those Days

Ironically, many of the men aboard the *William Torr* had earlier that season been rescued from the shipwreck of the *Dordon*.

The *William Torr* was never seen again. But evidence was found indicating that she had become a total wreck. The following year, in the middle of August, a ship returning to Britain from the Mediterranean found a large oil cask belonging to her. A pack of staves was found washed ashore in Shetland. A ship bound for Quebec found another oil cask from the lost ship in the Atlantic, and another cask containing blubber was picked up by a ship en route to Nova Scotia.

In 1840, the *Norfolk* was in Cumberland Sound, where Captain Harrison heard from Inuit about the wreck of a ship off Cape Fry some years earlier. The Inuit reported that the ship was frozen into the land ice and that they had gone out by sled to see her. But a gale from the southeast brought in heavy drift ice, which crushed her sides. Two of the masts fell towards the land; the other fell seaward.

Some of the crew, each carrying a bundle of clothing, set out over the ice on foot, hoping to reach the *Jane*, which they assumed was iced in somewhere to the south of them. Among these men, who were never seen again, was a man whom the natives said was short and red-faced, an apt description of Captain Smith. The other men, twenty-two in number, went ashore with the Inuit, who did their best to nurse them back to health. To a man, however, they were so badly frostbitten that none survived.

Some years later, the Shetlander who had been among the last to see the *William Torr* was in the same area. The Inuit offered to take the Shetlander and his fellow crew members inland, and he reported, "They would show us the graves of white men, which we supposed to be those of the *William Torr*." He noted that "a whale-ship next summer found a boat with seven corpses in her, on the ice. No doubt these were some of them also."

Thus ended the tragedy of the *William Torr.*

The Landmark Rock at Durban Harbour

When I was a very young man, I transferred from Qikiqtarjuaq (then Broughton Island) to the remote island of Padloping, as teacher in the one-room school there. (The Inuktitut spelling of the island's name is Paallakvik.) During my first year in the Arctic, I had already developed an insatiable interest in Northern history, and Inuit language and culture. Padloping, I thought, with its miniscule population of thirty-four, would give me an opportunity to increase my language skills and learn more about the North.

Padloping is a small island, about six or seven miles long and perhaps two miles wide, off the east coast of Baffin Island, about sixty-five miles south of Qikiqtarjuaq, on the edge of Davis Strait. Farther east is Greenland. I had with me a well-thumbed book,

The Norse Atlantic Saga by Gwyn Jones, which told of the ancient Norse settlements in Greenland, and their population, which had disappeared sometime near the middle of the last millennium. There was speculation that some of the lost settlers may have headed west, to Baffin Island.

The book had a few illustrations, and some were of a runic inscription found on the Greenland coast. One day, when Eliyah Qakulluk, a local hunter, was visiting me, he perused the book, looking carefully at the pictures—for he could not read English. He was a frequent visitor to my home, actually an apartment attached to the school, for the school with its appendages was the only building in the settlement that had electricity. Eliyah and others liked to visit, listen to my record player, and look at my books.

Eliyah gazed at the runic inscription. I asked him if he had ever seen anything like that in or around Padloping. He told me that he had—that there was a boulder bearing a similar inscription not far away.

I was excited. For some time, there had been stories about such an inscription on or near Padloping. One was that a white man in Padloping, in the days when the Unites States Air Force ran a weather station there, had found a rock with a runic inscription and turned it face down to preserve it. The story is likely apocryphal, but in any case, such a rock lying face down in the Arctic would never be found again.

But the rock that Eliyah described was different. He talked about a large boulder standing quite visible near the shoreline at a place called Kisarvik. Other men of the community confirmed his story. They showed me on a map where it was located—on an island about ten miles east of our village.

In Those Days

In the spring, when the light was good, Jacopie Kokseak, Simo Alookie, and Eliyah took me to see the rock that had had my interest all through the winter. I was filled with excitement, fully expecting that I was about to be the first modern-day *Qallunaaq* (white person) to discover, and reveal to an unsuspecting world, a runic inscription on the Canadian coast. *Discover*, of course, was a poor word to describe what I thought was about to happen, for the Inuit had always known about this boulder and its strange inscription.

We stopped our snowmobiles on the ice, and the Inuit pointed out the boulder onshore. It wasn't gigantic, but it was big enough to attract attention from the sea. If there was an inscription on it, then the boulder itself was clearly intended to be a landmark.

With my camera slung around my neck, I approached the rock, eager to document my find. As I got closer, I could see that an inscription had been cut deeply into the face of the rock. Numbers! And letters! But—what was this? They were English letters!

I was dismayed. This was not a runic inscription, I explained to Jacopie and the others. But what was it? And who could have carved it?

The Inuit had an explanation. The inscription was not in Inuktitut syllabics, so it had to have been done by a white man. They concluded that it must have been done by Sivutiksaq. But this served only to deepen the mystery. I had never heard the name Sivutiksaq before. He was apparently a Qallunaaq. But who was he?

There were no answers that day on the shores of Durban Harbour, only questions. The answers would have to wait. But when they came, they were significant.

* * *

On that spring day in 1968, I stood at Durban Harbour looking at a large boulder, photographing it from a number of angles and contemplating an inscription that someone had taken a great deal of time to carve.

The inscription began with the latitude and longitude: 67°1' N, followed by the longitude 62°20' W. I didn't have a map with me at the time, but as it turns out, this position is not accurate, but fairly close to the actual location of the boulder. These coordinates place the boulder on Block Island, a little west of its actual location. Still, considering when it was carved, I was impressed.

Below that was a line of letters: a *T* followed by a superscript *R,* and then the line *J G P H D.* Some of these letters are separated by periods. Underneath that was a line that gave a date: *J* followed by a superscript *Y* (an abbreviation for July), followed by *17,* and then *1837.*

I concluded that someone had been there on July 17, 1837, and taken considerable trouble to leave a permanent record of his presence. The Inuit call the harbour Kisarvik, and the word provides a clue, for it means "the anchorage." I thought it likely that a man from a whaling ship had done this work. But who? And why?

I began to research the life of the mysterious white man Sivutiksaq, and learned that he was William Duval, a whaler who had arrived in the North in the late 1870s at the age of twenty-one. He had lived in or near Durban Harbour at one point in his colourful life, but he could not have been the author of the mysterious inscription.

When I got my pictures developed, I sent one to the Scott Polar Research Institute in Cambridge, England, asking them if there was a scholar there who could shed any light on the inscription.

In Those Days

Happily, there was. In due course, I received a letter from Gil Ross, who was researching Canadian Arctic whaling.

He was able to provide an interpretation of the letters on the third line of the boulder. He wasn't sure what *TR* meant, but *JG* meant *Joseph Green*, the name of a whaling ship. *PHD* was an abbreviation for Peterhead, the port in northeastern Scotland that the ship had sailed from. By good fortune, the log of the *Joseph Green* for 1837 still existed, in an archive in Britain, and it confirmed that the vessel was indeed in Durban Harbour on the date in question.

It seems that, in fact, Durban Harbour was a popular spot for whalers. Ships often put in there to take on water and to trade with the Inuit. The Inuktitut name, Kisarvik, was a reminiscence of those distant days when whaling was important in their lives.

But why all the effort to inscribe the latitude and longitude into this boulder in a small bay in an isolated part of the Arctic? The answer may be tied up with the search for an accurate method of determining longitude at sea, important for navigators. (The calculation of latitude was relatively easy.) To calculate the longitude, mariners needed to know the precise time. But pendulum clocks did not work very well at sea, because of the pitching and rolling of ships and the pounding of wind and waves. It was not until the invention of marine chronometers that longitude could be accurately calculated. However, chronometers were extremely expensive, and not all ships could carry them. It is doubtful that many whaling ships in the first half of the 1800s could do so. If the *Joseph Green* did, that could have enabled someone of its crew to calculate the longitude at the popular anchorage at Durban Harbour and inscribe it on the prominent boulder near the shore.

If Durban Harbour were to become a reference point for navigation in Davis Strait—think of it as a prime meridian for that area—this would assist accurate celestial navigation in the strait. It could also be used to temporarily reset such clocks as whaling ships carried and thereby calculate more or less accurate time.

This is my conjecture, after discussions with friends who know far more about navigation than I do, as to why men from the *Joseph Green* would make the effort to carve their position into a boulder in an isolated harbour in 1837. And once they had done so, we have no idea how long the rock served the purpose for which it was intended. Today it remains an isolated curiosity, seldom seen and known only to a few.

Inuluapik and Penny Discover Cumberland Sound

In 1839, William Penny, a veteran Scottish whaler, made a fortuitous stop at Durban Island on the Baffin coast. It was a favoured spot for whalers to take on water and to trade with the Inuit who congregated there increasingly in the 1830s.

Whalers had exploited the waters of Davis Strait for over a century, but it was only since 1817 that they had made the dangerous crossing of Baffin Bay to harvest the bowhead whale on the virgin eastern coast of Baffin Island. The bowhead was also known as the Greenland right whale, because it was the "right" whale to hunt. It was slow-moving, huge, and generally floated when killed, leading to relatively few losses of struck whales. But nonetheless, whaling was a dangerous business. In 1819, ten ships were lost in Baffin Bay. In 1830, ninety-one British ships sailed for

Davis Strait, but the weather that year was unusually fierce, and nineteen of those ships were lost. Of those that did return to port, many were badly damaged and had poor catches to show for their efforts. Five years later, only six ships were lost, but eleven were trapped by ice, and six hundred men had to winter in the Arctic unprepared for the severity of the winter. Of those 600, 135 froze to death or died of scurvy.

Into this unpromising situation stepped William Penny. He wanted to search for the elusive Cumberland Sound, mapped by John Davis in the 1580s but never entered since. At Durban Island, Inuit had told him of a large inlet to the south, an inlet they called Tinujjiarvik. The Inuit said that it was rich with bowhead whales and other wildlife. Penny supposed that Tinujjiarvik and Cumberland Sound were one and the same. He thought it might prove to be a profitable hunting ground for the bowhead, which was already becoming scarce elsewhere.

In 1839, after fishing in Baffin Bay, Penny made for Durban Island. There he met Inuluapik,[1] a young Inuit man in his late teens or early twenties, who seemed to know a great deal about the much-reported Tinujjiarvik. He had been born at Qimmiqsut, an island on the southern coast of that body of water. Earlier in that decade, his family had moved to the Davis Strait coast precisely because they had heard that whalers frequented the area, and Inuluapik's father foresaw the possibility of acquiring trade goods from them.

Inuluapik drew a sketch for Penny. Although he had not seen Cumberland Sound for many years, his map was drawn

---

[1] Contemporary sources spell Inuluapik's name in a variety of ways, but the most common was Eenoolooapik. I have chosen to render it in the current Inuktitut phonemic orthography.

in considerable detail. It so impressed Penny that he invited the young man to accompany him to Aberdeen to spend the winter and return with him again the following year. Penny's motivation was purely self-serving. With the assistance of Inuluapik, he hoped to gain publicity and government support for a purely exploratory voyage the following year to find the elusive entrance to Tinujjiarvik, and thereby rediscover Cumberland Sound.

Inuluapik was not concerned with whether or not he was being exploited. This was the opportunity he had been waiting for. In previous years, he had begged whaling captains to take him to Scotland but had found none willing. Now, with the consent of his friends and relatives, and despite the tears of his mother, Inuluapik eagerly accepted Penny's invitation. His mother, fearing that she would never see her son again, exposed her breast for him to suckle one last time, as he had done in his youth. This farewell completed, Inuluapik boarded the *Neptune* sometime in October 1839 and entrusted himself to the care of William Penny.

The ship reached Aberdeen on November 8. Inuluapik's arrival created a sensation. It also nearly cost him his life, for he caught a lung infection almost immediately. Some days later, at Penny's suggestion, he gave a demonstration of his kayaking ability on the River Dee. Although it was a warm fall day, he performed in full fur dress. The result was a recurrence of his lung ailment. This time he was confined to bed for fourteen days. His health remained poor for the rest of his stay in Britain.

Inuluapik's trip to Scotland was the first of many to be made by Inuit from Baffin Island across the Atlantic during the next three quarters of a century while whaling flourished.

* * *

Inuluapik and Penny left Aberdeen aboard a different ship, the *Bon Accord*, on April 1. After a difficult crossing of the North Atlantic, they reached Davis Strait on May 5. The government had failed to provide any funds for a purely exploratory voyage, so Penny headed north to whale in Melville Bay, and eventually headed south to search for Tinujjiarvik.

On July 27, near Leopold Island, the *Bon Accord* encountered the unexpected—the land seemed to end abruptly, reappearing to the south at an apparent distance of sixty or seventy miles. They had arrived at the mouth of an enormous inlet. Could this be Tinujjiarvik? Could it be Davis's long-lost Cumberland Sound? Penny thought it must be.

Inuluapik had described Tinujjiarvik as teeming with *arviit*—the bowhead whales that were the prize sought after by Arctic whalers. He confirmed Penny's supposition. This was indeed Tinujjiarvik. But Penny checked his maps and his latitude carefully and changed his mind. He concluded incorrectly that this inlet was in the wrong place to be Cumberland Sound—in the years since Davis had first entered the sound, and in the absence of new information over two and a half centuries, cartographers had moved it around considerably on their maps. Penny decided that it must be something altogether new. He named it Hogarth's Sound, in honour of the owner of his previous ship, the *Neptune*. It would be a few years before the error was recognized and the original name restored.

Ice prevented an immediate entry to the inlet, but eventually a southeast breeze dispersed it. On August 2, Penny hailed two nearby ships, the *Lady Jane* of Newcastle and the *Lord Gambier* of Hull, which followed him into the sound. They followed the northeast shoreline and eventually met two Inuit, who came aboard Penny's ship. Inuluapik told them about his adventures in the white man's land. They promised him that they would pass on the news of his return to other Inuit, so that his mother might be informed.

Finally, the ships crossed the sound to Qimmiqsut, Inuluapik's birthplace. Offshore, they met a group of Inuit, two of whom were the young man's cousins. One might well wonder what would be the first of all his experiences the young traveller would relate to impress his relatives. Surprisingly, he didn't tell initially about any of his experiences in Scotland. Instead he told of meeting Inuit on the Greenland coast and described the peculiar way in which they spoke. He also demonstrated the use of a gun that Captain Penny had given him as a gift during his long convalescence in Scotland.

Penny insisted that Inuluapik not leave the ship at Qimmiqsut but rather accompany him farther into the sound. He was concerned that they still had not seen any whales. At the head of the sound, the *Bon Accord* anchored in a harbour near the Inuit village of Nulluk. The next day, in the ship's boat, Penny set out on an exploratory voyage to the last long arm of Cumberland Sound, now called Clearwater Fiord. He was accompanied by Inuluapik and an old man named Aaniapik. Inuluapik wanted to impress the old fellow, for on the previous day he had received the man's permission to marry his adopted daughter, Kunuk. In mid-August they returned from their search for whales, so far unsuccessful. Penny was beginning to despair, but the Inuit informed him that whales would be numerous in the fall.

Back at Qimmiqsut, Inuluapik left the ship. Penny headed for the mouth of the sound to check ice conditions. When he returned to Qimmiqsut, he was surprised to learn that Inuluapik had already disappeared inland on a hunting trip. He was even more startled to learn that he had already taken a wife—and it was not Kunuk.

Penny crossed again to the northern coast of the sound. Finally, he found whales, but luck was not with him. His crew only managed to harpoon two, and they were both lost. The *Bon Accord* left the sound on September 22 without catching a single whale.

Thus the voyage, which was of the most profound significance to the development of whaling in southern Baffin Island, although an exploratory success, was a financial disaster. The *Bon Accord* had been the only whaling ship remaining in Aberdeen, and her owner, a Mr. Crombie, was forced to sell her.

In the following years, Cumberland Sound became the most important whaling ground in the Canadian Arctic. Inuluapik quite literally put Cumberland Sound back on the map. The chart he prepared for Penny in 1839 bore a close resemblance to the map Penny prepared the following year. In that peculiar way white men have of looking at discovery, Inuluapik had helped a man rediscover something he had known was there all along.

Over-Wintering

The First Winter
in Cumberland Sound

T he winter of 1851–52 was one that changed forever the
lives of the Inuit of Cumberland Sound. It was a year of
hardship, like most years, but the Inuit were inured to
hardship. However, it was also the first year that white men wintered among the Inuit of the sound. Captain William Quayle of
the *McLellan*, sailing out of New London, Connecticut, left fourteen men to winter on Qimmiqsut, an island on the southwestern
shore of the sound. His hope was that this shore party would get
a head start on whaling at the floe edge the following spring, before a ship could normally reach the place. The man left in charge
of the party was a resourceful whaler in whom Captain Quayle
had a great deal of faith—Sidney O. Budington.

The party was left with scant provisions, for the vessel had
been supplied only for a normal whaling voyage. The men built a

house of stones and filled the crevices with moss and earth; poles covered with canvas formed a roof. With a dwelling secure, they turned their attention to the urgent matter of food. A member of the wintering party wrote: "Before winter was over we got very short of food, and could not have survived if it had not been for the game we shot and the seals we caught. We had to learn the Esquimaux way of eating and cooking, and before spring I was pretty well acclimated."

The following summer, the *McLellan* was crushed by ice in Baffin Bay before she could return to Cumberland Sound. Her crew was rescued in Davis Strait by Captain Parker of the famous whaler *Truelove*. With the *McLellan*'s crew aboard, Parker made for Cumberland Sound to pick up the fourteen men who had wintered. But he found no sailors when he reached Qimmiqsut. Fearing the worst, he continued up the sound and found the party of Americans safely ensconced at Neubuyan. They had thrived during the winter and had maintained friendly relations with the Inuit. William Barron, a crew member of the *Truelove*, described the situation: "The Americans were all quite well, and had not had a day's sickness. They had lived upon Esquimaux food, which is raw frozen seal or walrus flesh. . . . They had filled all their casks with oil, and killed several whales for the whalebone.... They had got so used to the native living that they almost preferred it to civilised food."

Barron commented further: "The Americans and natives were very intimate with each other, for during the whole twelve months they had been on the most friendly terms."

The *Truelove* spent much of that summer in Cumberland Sound. Barron was a young whaler, on his fourth voyage to Davis Strait. He already had a little experience working with and trading among the Inuit, on both sides of the strait, and was quite impressed with the Inuit he met in the sound. "The natives were the cleanest I had ever seen," he wrote. "Their dresses were very fancifully decorated with beads, and they had the most beautiful seal skins, which were also very clean. The young female natives wore dried salmon skin covered boots, which shone like silver when the sun was out."

When it came time for the Americans to leave aboard the *True-love*, he wrote, "the Americans and natives seemed very loth [*sic*] to leave each other, having been so long accustomed to each other's society. . . . All the natives came on board to take a last farewell of their American friends and our crew. They were very downhearted and crying. I believe it would have taken some of our friends very little persuasion to stay another winter."

One of the many Inuit who had met the American whalers was Tookoolito, who would go on, a decade later, to become interpreter for the explorer Charles Francis Hall. She was in her early teens when she met the wintering whalers. Until this time, she had probably only gone by her native name. But whalers seldom took the trouble to learn how to pronounce Inuit names; it was easier to simply give them white names. It was during this winter that the Americans gave her the name of Hannah, "on account of her native name being too long."

William Barron remarked in his memoirs that he met Hannah in Cumberland Sound in 1852. She and another young woman named Kukuya, and a boy nicknamed Monkey Jack by the whalers—probably Miqqusaaq—helped to teach Barron some of the Inuktitut language. "During our stay amongst the natives, I was enabled to speak the Esquimaux language," he wrote, "and it was very useful to me whilst sailing to that country."

Captain Parker was, as Barron noted, "a strict disciplinarian." No Inuit were allowed on board after dark; they were allowed to stay until the crew had had their tea, and then they were sent ashore. It is just as well for young Hannah that this was the practice, for a young lady such as she would have been attractive to a whaler far from home.

That first wintering was a successful one for the Americans, a harbinger of many winters to come, for Americans, English, and Scots began very soon to winter in the sound as a matter of course. But that winter and those following were less successful for the Inuit, even as the ships began to employ them in large numbers. "The greatest drawback was provisions," Barron wrote. "Many natives died through hunger during the winter, as they never provided for the future."

Near the end of the century, as an old man putting the adventures of his youth to paper, Barron came to the conclusion that Inuit had not benefited from their close interactions with whalers. He remarked, "It was very detrimental to the habits of the poor things, as their children were not then trained in the use of the bow and arrow or canoe, but trusted to the ships coming. They had got the habit of drinking rum and smoking tobacco, and had contracted other vices. . . . They were much better off while in their wild state."

A Whaling Captain, a Discovery Ship, and the White House Desk

A young boy peers out from under an ornate desk while his father works. The boy is John F. Kennedy Jr., affectionately known in his childhood as John-John. His famous father is the thirty-fifth president of the United States of America. The desk is magnificent, measuring six feet in length and four feet in width. But it is much more than an impressive piece of furniture. It is a token of the friendship that exists between two nations. It was fashioned by British craftsmen from wood taken from the hulk of a ship once salvaged at sea by an American whaler, as a gift for an earlier American president. Here is the story of that ship and that desk.

In 1852, a fleet of five ships left England to continue the search for the lost expedition of Sir John Franklin. The expedition was under the command of Sir Edward Belcher, who himself commanded one of the ships.

Captain Henry Kellett, in command of the *Resolute*, passed through Lancaster Sound and on to Melville Island, where he wintered at Dealy Island. The following summer, ice conditions were difficult, and the *Resolute* was unable to return very far eastward. Kellett had no choice but to winter again, this time off Bathurst Island.

In the spring of 1854, Edward Belcher controversially ordered the abandonment of all of the ships under his command except for the *North Star*, which had remained at Beechey Island as a floating supply depot. He and all the crews returned home in her and two other supply ships that arrived that summer. Thus began the incredible saga of the *Resolute*.

Abandoned on May 13, 1854, against the wishes of Captain Kellett, she drifted with the ice eastward through Lancaster Sound and south into Baffin Bay and Davis Strait. Sixteen months later, on September 10, 1855, a veteran whaling master, Captain James Buddington, on the whaling barque *George Henry*, sailing out of New London, Connecticut, was himself trapped in dense ice off the coast of eastern Baffin Island, south of present-day Qikiqtarjuaq. He sighted a ship some distance off and thought she might be an abandoned vessel. But ice conditions prevented him from checking out the situation immediately. Six days after sighting her, the two ships were still seven miles apart. He sent four men over the ice to investigate the ghost ship.

In Those Days

When they returned, they reported to Buddington that it was Her Britannic Majesty's ship *Resolute*.

A salvage at sea was potentially valuable. Buddington was elated. The *Resolute* was free of water and largely undamaged. Buddington himself took charge of her and, with a small crew, sailed her back to New London. His only navigational aids were an untrustworthy compass and an outline of the North American coast drawn on a single sheet of foolscap. The water tanks had burst, making the ship very light and prone to an exaggerated roll in heavy seas. At one point, the ship was storm-driven almost to Bermuda.

Buddington arrived in New London with his prize on Christmas Eve. The British government, notified of the find, formally waived all claim to the vessel. The United States Congress then took an unusual action. It purchased the *Resolute* for $40,000 from Buddington's employer. Buddington himself never saw any of the money, although he did arrange for some to be paid to his crew. The *Resolute* was moved to Brooklyn Navy Yard and repaired with the utmost care to make her fit for Arctic service once again. The United States government then made the unprecedented gesture of formally presenting the restored ship to "the Queen and people of Great Britain."

By the fall of 1856, all was ready. On the thirteenth of November, Captain Hartstein of the United States Navy sailed the restored ship out of New York and headed across the Atlantic. The crossing was uneventful. She reached Spithead and was towed to Cowes on the Isle of Wight, where she lay by the royal anchorage at Trinity Wharf. Queen Victoria arrived soon after. With the flags of both nations flying above the *Resolute*, on December 17, Captain Hartstein presented the vessel to Britain with these words: "Allow me to welcome your Majesty on board the *Resolute*, and, in obedience to the will of my countrymen and of the President of the United States, to restore her to you, not only as an evidence of a friendly feeling to your sovereignty, but as a token of love, admiration, and respect to your Majesty personally."

The Queen responded with a gracious smile and the words, "I thank you, Sir."

With the symbolic transfer over, the formal transfer happened two weeks later, on December 30. But the amazing story of the *Resolute* was not yet at an end.

The ship never returned to the Arctic. Instead, and amazingly, the Admiralty eventually ordered their gift dismantled. In 1879, she was reduced to a ghastly hulk. But remembering America's gift of two decades earlier, Queen Victoria ordered that a desk be constructed from the *Resolute*'s timbers. In an act of reciprocity and graciousness, the queen sent this desk as a gift to President Rutherford B. Hayes "as a memorial of the courtesy and loving kindness which dictated the offer of the gift of the *Resolute*."

Thus, a piece of the *Resolute* crossed the Atlantic once again. The magnificent desk sits in the Oval Office in the White House today. In the famous picture of young John Kennedy, son of President John F. Kennedy, peering out from under his father's desk, it is the *Resolute* desk he is under.

And on February 15, 1965, British prime minister Harold Wilson presented the bell of the *Resolute* to President Lyndon B. Johnson.

In Canada, the ship is remembered in the name of a small Inuit community and scientific staging point on Cornwallis Island.

The *Diana*, a Charnel House of Dead and Dying Men

Disasters were common in Davis Strait in the whaling days of the 1800s. Many ships were beset in the ice, and unprepared crews were forced to spend long winters of privation in the Arctic. Those iced in near land could occasionally rely on help from Inuit, but most winterings were far from shore. In many seasons, the loss of life was huge.

One of the greatest tragedies in Arctic whaling occurred on a whaling ship sent out from Hull, England, in 1866. She was the *Diana*, a steam whaler, and her captain, John Gravill, was a veteran of fifty years in the whaling business. But his experience was of little help in that desperate year.

In May, Captain Gravill put in at Lerwick in Shetland to hire the rest of his crew. With fifty men, thirty of them Shetlanders, he made for Davis Strait and its farthest northern reaches, Baffin Bay. In company with other whalers—the *Narwhal,* the *Esquimaux,* the *Intrepid,* and the *Truelove*—the *Diana* made her way through the pack ice of the bay to the North Water, where she took two whales, which would eventually be valued at £2,050. Later, the *Diana* and ten other ships were trapped by heavy ice near Pond Inlet. Eventually she was able to struggle southwards. With little fuel left, the crew burned everything that would burn, including many of the ship's spars. But on September 21, the ship was firmly beset off Clyde River, imprisoned in the ice there, and with only two months' provisions remaining.

For the next six months, the ship zigzagged southwards in the grip of the ice.

Christmas on a whaling ship locked in the ice, far from home, with provisions running low, was a particularly grim affair. The surgeon, Charles Smith, left a heart-rending account of Christmas Day on the *Diana*:

> I spent the entire night with the captain, who was extremely restless and uneasy. The weather during the night was horribly cold in the cabin.
>
> At 8 A.M. I went on deck, and found the ship driving with great rapidity towards a large iceberg. We passed within three or four ship's lengths of the berg. We were most wonderfully preserved from driving upon it or being crushed by the whirling, crashing ice, which was in commotion far and wide around the berg, which is aground.
>
> This morning the men held a prayer meeting in the

In Those Days

half-deck, and, it being Christmas Day, they commenced with singing the chant, "How beautiful upon the mountains."

Flour and plums having been served out yesterday, Joe, the cook, was up at three o'clock this morning, busy as a bee making plum puddings for the different messes. Every man and boy on board had a large slice of very good plum pudding served out to him at twelve o'clock in honour of Christmas Day. As most of the men have been saving up meat, biscuits, etc., you may be sure every one of our ships company enjoyed a good dinner. In the cabin we dined at one o'clock, and had a large plum pudding, which was equally divided, our usual three quarters of a pound of boiled salt beef, and a dish of tripe. George Clarke, the mate, had brought this, pickled in a jar, from home, and it turned out to be fearfully salt.

We ate our Christmas dinner almost in silence, each man's mind being occupied with gloomy thoughts of home, families, and friends. The poor old dying captain lay upon the sofa, occasionally turning over or dozing uneasily in a half-unconscious slumber.

What a Christmas dinner! What thoughts of the many merry ones at Sandon, and at home, and of last year's Christmas at Mister Moffatt's. What a change! Thoughts of father, brothers, and sisters, at home on Christmas Day, and thinking of me, as I am thinking of them.

To these thoughts add my anxieties and apprehensions on the captain's account, and the gloomy prospect before every one of us. You will readily believe that a more miserable Christmas dinner would be difficult to imagine even. The dinner, such as it was, was soon dispatched, and I was glad when 'twas over, it seems such a horrible mockery of the spirit of an English Christmas.

At about 3 P.M. the ice was in motion again, and pressing heavily upon the ship. I happened to be on deck at the time, but instantly ran down to the cabin. Here I found the captain, whom I had left calm and tranquil and breathing regularly, changed for the worse in a sudden and alarming manner.

He had heard or felt the ship move under the pressure of the ice, and knew very well what it meant. He knew that the ship was in danger. He knew, whatever poor chance his ship's company had of saving their lives, he had none if the ship were stove in and we had to take to the ice.

Happily, the pressure moderated and the ice became quieter. At 6 P.M. the captain was calmer but evidently very much weaker, and more incoherent and difficult to understand.[1]

The next day, Captain Gravill died. His body was not consigned to the sea, but rather was sewn in canvas and placed on the quarter deck. In the weeks that followed, half the crew was ravaged by scurvy. The living quarters were encased in ice.

A survivor recalled:

Our beef got done in January; coffee and sugar about that time also; and our last tea was served out in the beginning of February. Tobacco was likewise all gone, and some of us tried to smoke tea leaves and coffee grounds. The tea leaves burned the mouth bad, but the coffee grounds were not so

---

[1] Charles Edward Smith, *From the Deep of the Sea* (New York: The Macmillan Company, 1923), 174–75.

disagreeable. I do assure you it was precious cold—especially at night, when your breath froze in the top of your berth, till the ice came to be three or four inches thick, and we had a day every week to break it off and scrape it down with the ship's scrapers. . . . The men began to get down-hearted, and some of them were so weak that they dropped at the pumps.[2]

In mid-March in southern Davis Strait, the ship was finally released from the ice and began a race against death across the Atlantic, leaking badly all the while.

On April 2, she limped into Ronas Voe, an inlet on the west side of Shetland. The captain and eight other seamen lay dead on deck, and four more men were breathing their last. The remaining men were so weak that only three could go aloft to stow the sails when she anchored. One man is said to have dropped dead in shock at the sight of land. One report described the *Diana*, while anchored in Ronas Voe, as "a charnel house of scurvy-stricken, dysentery-worn, dead and dying men."

The ship took on a new crew in Shetland and continued on to Hull, reaching her home port on April 26 after an absence of fourteen months. She was repaired and returned to whaling. Two years later, the last whaler to sail from the port of Hull, she sank.

Many of the dead from that disastrous 1866 voyage were Shetlanders, and in 1890, the surgeon's brother had a large memorial fountain erected near the harbour in Lerwick. It bears the words: "In Memory of the Providential Return of the S. [Steam] Whaler

---

[2]Anonymous, "Arrival of the Missing Whaleship 'Diana,' and Dreadful Sufferings of the Crew," *The Nautical Magazine and Naval Chronical,* vol. 36 (May 1867): 281.

Diana of Hull." It's hard to miss. At the edge of a parking lot at the dock, a few steps from the town centre, it keeps the tragedy of the *Diana* alive in the minds of Shetlanders. It is still spoken about, an integral part of Shetland's history, and a symbol of the fate of many island men who went to the Arctic whaling.

May Day
on a Whaler

A tradition developed on Scottish whaling ships to the Arctic that crew members making their first trip—"green hands," as they were called—had to be initiated to the rigours of the North. A similar tradition existed on merchant ships crossing the equator. On Arctic ships, the ceremony—which for some curious reason lost to time was known as "the double mess pot"—took place on the first of May. The ships had usually left Scotland in April, and by May 1 they were usually at or near the ice edge in Davis Strait. Whether they were or not, that is the day the ceremony was celebrated.

On May Day, sailors would open small packets of ribbon that their sweethearts had given them when they left their home port. The ribbons were knotted, and each knot represented a whale that the loved one back home hoped her man would help to catch. The men would count the knots. But to open the package and count them before May Day would bring bad luck to the entire ship.

On the same day, men would produce bits of ribbon that they had snipped from the hats and dresses of women back home and fashion these into garlands, in the centre of which they would add good-luck charms, even small models of the ship. These would be raised to the mast, where they would remain until the vessel returned home, by which time the garlands were bleached white.

The initiation ceremony for the green hands was often gruesome, even cruel, and green hands often lived in fear of it until the day it happened. Alex Trotter described part of it in 1856:

This morning, immediately after 12 o'clock, a curious ceremony was gone through on board. . . . About 10 minutes past the midnight hour, although it was clear as mid-day, I was startled by the sound of a horn blazing three loud blasts and on looking up I beheld two strangely-attired figures leaping over the bows of the vessel, not however, before a voice had thundered, "Ship ahoy," which words had been set to music by the ringing of bells.

The one figure was the great Neptune; the other was his wife. Their appearance was very remarkable. Let me describe the nobler animal first: his headpiece bore a striking resemblance to a red nightcap such as human beings wear; his face was covered with a beautiful veil which, however, allowed his beard, white as the coat of polar bear, to fall gracefully down on his breast; his habitments were first, covering the crown of his head to the waist and including his arms, an Esquimaux coat made out of seal skins and sewn together with sinews of the whale; second, his . . .

trousers were also made of sealskins, which is very natural as what else could the so-called God of the sea get to clothe himself with? In one hand he carried a trident, an emblem of his authority, and in the other the trumpet through which he had summoned our vessel. His beloved loving spouse was attired in a pair of moleskin trousers and was otherwise wrapped up in a large green shawl.[1]

These two crewmen, dressed up as Mr. and Mrs. Neptune, were accompanied by burly servants carrying long lances. The green hands were blindfolded and subjected to a cruel ceremony. First, each was asked to kiss Mrs. Neptune. But, unknown to them, a mixture of gunpowder and flour was placed in front of them, a lighted candle beside it. As Mrs. Neptune blew her kiss, this mixture ignited and set fire to the green hand's whiskers. Then a frothy mixture of oil, soot, and grease would be shoved in his mouth and lathered onto his face. His burned chin would be shaved with a primitive razor made from a hoop saw. Properly humiliated, he would then be saluted as a freeman of "Greenland."

Some reports say that Mrs. Neptune sometimes kissed the blindfolded sailors while wearing a moustache made of nail points.

There was one way out of this barbaric rite, but common sailors could not afford it. It was to bribe the royal sea couple with a suitable gift, and nothing was more acceptable than a bottle of rum. This was what the ship's surgeons and visiting explorers

---

[1] Innes Macleod, *To the Greenland Whaling: Alexander Trotter's Journal of the Voyage of the Enterprise in 1856 from Fraserburgh & Lerwick* (Sandwich, Shetland: The Thule Press, 1979), 39.

usually did. Arthur Conan Doyle, who travelled as surgeon on the *Hope* in 1880, successfully bribed his way out of the ceremony.

Shipboard etiquette was often suspended for May Day. The royal couple, nothing more than crew members in costume, could address the captain directly and even demand a cup of grog in his cabin. The day usually ended with a "mollie," as the Dundee whalers called it—a party with singing and dancing and music from bagpipes or a melodeon.

Words from
the Whalers

Borrowed Words

A century ago, when bowhead whaling was still an important industry in the waters off Canada's eastern Arctic, Inuit and whites were faced with the problem of communicating with each other. Many of the whalers who returned year after year learned to speak Inuktitut, as did the traders who followed them. In fact, of the few white people who lived in the Canadian Arctic in those far-off days, probably a larger percentage spoke Inuktitut than do now. Many Inuit—especially men who formed the crews of local whaleboats—also learned to speak English well, and others learned a kind of trade jargon that was a mixture of both languages.

But the whalers who came to the Arctic did not all speak the same kind of English—some were American, some were English, and some were Scottish. And even among the Scots, there was a variety of dialects, with those from Dundee speaking very differently than those from Peterhead.

Sometimes Inuit borrowed words from English and took them into their own language, often modifying their pronunciations to suit the sound requirements of Inuktitut. Over time some of the words have passed out of common usage in English, so that a "loan word" in Inuktitut is not always recognizable as such.

I'll give a few examples.

In some Inuit communities, the word for a cup is *panika* or *panikak*. In others, it is *irngusiq*. Most people, whether white or Inuit, do not realize that the first word is of English origin. It is the mostly forgotten English word *pannikin*, which referred to a metal mug with a handle. Inuit acquired pannikins from English or Scottish whalers as trade goods. In the 1880s, the anthropologist Franz Boas, in describing the fall festival of the Inuit in Cumberland Sound, writing about the tug-of-war competition between those born in the summer and those born in the winter, wrote, "Then the rope was laid down. A large tin pot was placed in the middle and the women brought some water from every house in pannikins." Forgotten in English, the word survives today in Inuktitut.

Another word, the origin of which may be obscure, is the word generally pronounced as *uasakua*, often with a slight hint of a *t* at the end. This is a word used in some eastern Inuktitut dialects to describe a vest. The word comes from the English word *waistcoat*, which—for reasons known only to the British—is pronounced *wescot*. Inuit took the British pronunciation and modified it to suit their own needs.

An even more obscure example is a word that today is used to describe a servant, or a person who is subservient to another person. The word is *siala*. It comes, strangely enough, from the English word *sailor*. Think about it. In whaling days, a ship had a captain and sailors. The captain was referred to in Inuktitut by the borrowed term *kapitan* or *kapitai*. But the word for sailor required some modification. It became *siala*. As whaling transformed itself into trading, many Inuit became dependent on the traders at the shore stations for ammunition, tobacco, and some food items. The traders described these Inuit as their "sailors." In a fascinating description of the general rules that governed trade between Inuit and whites, the missionary E. W. T. Greenshield wrote, "When a trader says to a native in the fall, 'You are going to be my sailor,' and gives him his pay in kind, the man is in his service throughout the ensuing fall, winter, and spring."

Sailor in this context shows up many times in the testimony gathered from Inuit about the murder of Robert Janes in 1920 near Arctic Bay. Inuit who had refused to trade with Janes—there were two other traders in the area—were quoted as telling Janes, "I am not your sailor." The word survives today with the meaning of "servant" or "a subservient person."

Husky: The Evolution of a Term for Inuit

Everyone knows the word *husky* as a name used for the dogs that Inuit and other Northerners use to haul sleds. And everyone knows the adjective *husky* describes someone who is stocky or robust. Most would think that the two words are related, especially since the husky dogs are known to be strong and tireless.

But, in fact, the two terms are not related at all. The adjective *husky* is derived from the word *husk*, the dry and often tough outer covering of some foods, like corn. The *Oxford English Dictionary* defines *husky* as "tough and strong (like a corn-husk); big, strong, and vigorous."

It is simply a coincidence that the husky dog is also tough, strong, and vigorous. The derivation of the word is quite different.

When white explorers and whalers first encountered Inuit in the Arctic, they didn't use the word *Inuit* to name them. Rather, they used a word that is generally said to have been borrowed from a First Nations language, the word that came to be standardized in French as *Esquimau* (*Esquimaux* in the plural) and *Eskimo* in English. Its meaning was said to be "eaters of raw meat." But the word had many variations before it finally settled down into the English or French forms that became standard.

Arctic literature abounds with various permutations of the word. Consider these:

In 1743, James Isham, writing about his time in Hudson Bay, used the spelling *Ehuskemay*. In a word list that he compiled on an expedition in the late 1870s, Heinrich Klutschak noted the word *eisiki* as meaning "man." The engineer of the whaleship *Camperdown* wrote in 1861 that Inuit men were called *Ossaki* on the Baffin coast. Other variations were *Uskimay*, *Usquemows*, and *Uskees* (certainly a short form).

The addition of the initial *h* may have been a dialectal innovation from England or even Newfoundland. Some English and Newfoundland dialects add the consonant *h* at the beginning of a word starting with a vowel. In 1924, Mason wrote that "Esquimaux" were called "Huskemaw" in Labrador. *Husky* was almost certainly an abbreviation of this word or one of its variants. In 1830, an observer wrote of northern Quebec, "There was a cry that the river was full of Hoskies (Esquimaux)." A magazine article in 1889 noted that "The Indians were terribly afraid of the Esquimaux, who up there are called Huskeys." Alpheus Spring Packard, an American entomologist, writing of Labrador in 1891, referred to "the Eskimos, by whalers called 'Huskies.'"

Even Inuit used the word when talking with whalers or explorers. The much-maligned Greenlander Adam Beck, while himself maligning the abilities of the interpreter Carl Petersen, a Dane, told Charles Francis Hall, "Carl Petersen no speak Husky quick—not good Husky speak—small speak Husky!"

All of these terms were used for the people. How then did the name migrate from the people to the husky dog? Simple. The Huskies (the people) used dogs. They were the dogs of the Huskies, the Huskies' dogs, and eventually simply the husky dogs.

For a time, the two terms coexisted. Mason wrote in 1924, "On the Arctic tundras the 'Huskies' use long runner-sleds with the little short-legged 'husky' dogs who can run all day over the iron-like crusted snow."

But eventually the explorers' and whalers' name for the people became standardized as *Eskimo* (to later be replaced with *Inuit*), and the connection between the two words was generally forgotten.

Yakkie: A Scottish Word for Inuit

Whalers used a number of words to refer to Inuit. But perhaps the strangest word was *Yak,* or *Yakkie,* a term that has passed out of use, and out of general knowledge. References to this word are quite common in whaling literature. Here are a few examples.

Joseph Rene Bellot, writing about the search for Sir John Franklin, wrote, "Dr. Kane tells me that the scurvy appears occasionally among the Huskies, or Yacks, as they are still called, in consequence of the little variety in their food."

Benjamin Sharp, a participant on one of Robert Peary's expeditions to northwestern Greenland, made a distinction between what he said whalers called the Inuit of southern Greenland and what they called those of the far North. He wrote of a man he met, "He was a fine-looking fellow, this 'Yak,' as the whalemen call these Arctic Highlanders, in contra-distinction to the 'Huskie' of southern Greenland." I have not seen this distinction in any other source.

Bernard O'Reilly, in his strange work *Greenland, the Adjacent Seas, and the North-West Passage,* published in 1818, said (incorrectly) that *Yak* derived from *Uskee* (his version of *Huskie*). An anonymous reviewer, probably John Barrow, writing in the *Quarterly Review*, tore O'Reilly's work to shreds and lampooned him for his etymological guesswork, writing: "From Uskee comes (we know not how) yak, and from yak, yankee—of doodle Mr. O'Reilly says nothing."

The Greenlandic Inuit traveller John Sakeouse, on his deathbed in Scotland, referred to himself as a Yakkie. Other Inuit who worked closely with the whalers may have referred to themselves and their fellow countrymen as Yaks or Yakkies when talking with whalers. The Inuit camp Kivitoo, about forty miles north of Qikiqtarjuaq (Broughton Island), was known to all whalers simply as Yakkie Fiord. It was a popular place, where whaling ships would take on fresh water and meet with the Inuit, or Yakkies, to trade.

But where did this strange appellation come from? The answer is simple. Today, the English word *yack* is a verb meaning "to talk incessantly." But in the dialect of lowland Scots spoken by most of the whalers in the 1900s, it had a different meaning. It meant "to speak unintelligibly." (Whalers weren't generally well educated and so were not big on spelling, so the disappearance of the letter *c* from *yack* is irrelevant.) Of course, the language of the Inuit was unintelligible to most whalers. To them, the Inuit were "yacking." And so it was logical that they should be referred to as the Yakkies or Yaks.

Today, this strange word is unknown to anyone not familiar with the scattered writings left by the Scottish whalemen who visited the eastern Arctic.

Cooney: A Whaler Word for Woman and Wife

When the anthropologist Franz Boas spent a winter near Pangnirtung in 1883, he made the following observations in his diary: "A cooney is drying my stockings and kommings [*kamiit*, sealskin boots]." "Mutch's kuni is complaining of a sore ear." "In the morning Pakkak and his kuni were here, mapping Kignait [*sic*] and Padli for me." "In the morning I went to see the kuni."

What, one may well ask in the absence of any context to explain this word, is a cooney, or kuni?

It becomes more clear in the following excerpts. In 1871, as the Polaris expedition under Charles Francis Hall prepared to leave for northern Greenland and an attempt to reach the North Pole, a newspaper reported, "Two Esquimaux, Joe and his 'cooney,' or wife, Hannah . . . also go with the expedition, the former as the interpreter and the latter in the capacity as a tailoress."

In 1878, Frederick Schwatka led a small expedition north to the Kitikmeot region. One member of the expedition, Heinrich Klutschak, published a short Inuktitut vocabulary as part of his record of the expedition's two years in the North. On that list was the word *kuni*, with its meaning given (in translation from the German of Klutschak's original) as "woman."

It is obvious from the examples given that this strange word *cooney*, or *kuni*, was a word used by white men in referring to an Inuit woman or wife. What's not clear is why.

Let's look at a few more examples. Alex Smith was the engineer on the vessel *Camperdown* in 1861. He recorded that the Inuit men went by the term *ossaki* (a version of *Husky*), the women were *coonas*, and the children were *piccaninnies*. These words were in use at Pond Inlet and also at Clyde River.

Two years later, an illustration in a book on whaling carried the caption "Eskimo Coonah or female."

The word was even used on the Labrador coast. In 1892, the Hudson's Bay Company post manager at Davis Inlet mentioned in his journal that a ship had arrived with men trying to recruit Inuit to take to the World's Fair in Chicago: "Mr. Vincent and Capt. McConnel came down from the north this morning where they had anchored last night. They were trying to get Esquimaux & Cunis to take back to the United States for the World's Fair." In this example, *Cunis* is a variant spelling and plural.

Where did this curious term come from?

The word has now passed completely from use. Probably it hasn't been used for over a hundred years. It does not seem to have an origin in any Scottish dialect. Some have suggested that it comes from the root *kunik,* meaning "kiss." I doubt it. The whalers who used the word on the Baffin coast also fished on the eastern shores of Davis Strait. There they met the Inuit of Greenland and the few Danish administrators and traders who lived among them. The Danish word for *woman* or *wife* is *kone* (pronounced *koe-neh*). It is not much of a leap of faith to imagine the whalers subsequently pronouncing this word as *kuni* (*cooney*).

In fact, a variant of the word, which may have been borrowed by Inuit in southern Greenland as far back as Viking times, was recorded as "Kona: Agnak"—*Agnak* (today spelled *arnaq*) means "woman"—in a German-Greenlandic wordlist compiled by the Danish historian Peder Hansen Resen in 1654.

I suggest that the whalers learned this word on the Greenland coast and brought it to Baffin.

Portagee: The Inuktitut Word for Black Person

I am often asked: What is the origin of the word *Portagee,* or *Portugee?* The word sounds like it might be used to describe Portuguese people, and, in fact, some dialect dictionaries of English include an entry for *Portugee,* with the explanation that it is substandard English speech meaning "Portuguese." This doesn't help at all, however, to explain why it is used by Canadian Inuit—at least in the eastern Arctic—to describe black people.

The answer is to be found in the history of the whaling industry in the Arctic. American whalemen roamed the world in search of their cetacean prey. Often they augmented their crews with men from islands where they stopped for water, news, or supplies. One such place was the Cape Verde Islands.

The Cape Verde Islands is a group of islands in the mid-Atlantic about three hundred miles off the coast of Africa. It was discovered, uninhabited, by Portuguese navigators in the fifteenth century and, because of its location astride eventually important mid-Atlantic shipping lanes, it was colonized under Portuguese domination. Portugal played an important role in the trans-Atlantic slave trade, and so the islands came to have an African population as well as a European one. Eventually much of the population was Creole, that is, of mixed ancestry.

New England whaling ships made Cape Verde a regular port of call, and picked up crewmen there and on the west coast of Africa itself. These men, whether Cape Verdean or African, were usually Portuguese speakers and were identified by the whalers as Portuguese. The American shipowners, frugal businessmen, in fact preferred to recruit men in Cape Verde because the men there "worked hard to save what they could while on board the vessel and they could be hired for much less money than American seamen. Furthermore, they made a disciplined crew." The American captains were not averse to taking on escaped slaves and even criminals. But regardless of their origins, the Cape Verdeans were generally considered to be "hardworking, honest seamen." By the early years of the 1800s, three-eighths of the crewmen on Nantucket whaling ships were "coloured."

Eventually many Cape Verdeans settled in New England itself, especially in the area of New Bedford, Massachusetts. From there, many continued to work in whaling. Many were crew members of vessels that came to the eastern Arctic, where whaling was centred in Cumberland Sound and the Repulse Bay area. They would naturally have been described by other crew members as *Portugee* or *Portagee*—a standard mispronunciation of *Portuguese*—and may have self-identified as such. In this way, Inuit learned that these dark-skinned members of the whaling crews were different than the Qallunaat—the white men—on the ships. Inuit learned the word *Portugee* but modified the sounds a little to make it more easily pronounceable, the way Inuit have done with many words borrowed from other languages and cultures. In this case, the word became more like *Puatugi*. (Inuit readers may have other preferred ways of spelling it—I have written it here the way it would be written in standard Inuktitut phonemic orthography.)

Because whaling was a worldwide enterprise, the word became known in the western Canadian Arctic as well, where Herschel Island was an important whaling centre. In 1910, Vilhjalmur Stefansson quoted Natkusiak, an Alaskan Eskimo living in the western Canadian Arctic, as saying of the first Inuit they encountered farther east, "And one looks like a Portugee." R. M. Anderson on the Canadian Arctic Expedition described the former whaler Peter Lopez, who had married an Inuit woman, as "a Portuguese Negro." Many Inuit throughout the Arctic have Portagee (Puatugi) whalers among their ancestors.

In 1971, the author James Houston published his novel *The White Dawn*, based on an actual historical event that occurred in the eastern Arctic in the 1800s. Three men from a whaling ship ended up living with Inuit, initially on friendly terms, but eventually with tragic consequences. One was a black man. The only name he has in the book is Portagee. In the movie made of the story in 1974, his part was played by the African-American actor Lou Gossett Jr.

Sometimes one also hears the word *Qirniqtaq* to describe a black person. But it has not supplanted the use of *Portagee*.

This is the interesting history of a word still common in Inuktitut speech, but whose origins have been obscured by time.

Sivataaqvik: Biscuit Day

Although many of the whalers who came to the Canadian Arctic were rough-and-tumble types, a number of the ships' captains were devout Christian men who observed the Sabbath. On some ships, all work stopped at midnight on Saturday night and did not resume for twenty-four hours. Often the ship's doctor or the captain himself would conduct divine services.

The Inuit quickly learned which captains observed the Sabbath and which did not, though they can only have had a rudimentary idea of the reasons behind this forced and artificial abstinence from activity. Margaret Penny accompanied her husband, William Penny, a well-known whaling master, on a wintering voyage to Cumberland Sound in 1857. Penny observed the Sabbath, and Margaret recorded in her journal for Sunday, October 11, that six or seven whales were seen, and that divine service was held at 2:00 P.M. She wrote, "The Esquimaux seem to understand very well that they are to respect this day, for they go about very quietly & forego their usual occupations."

For the Inuit, time had been governed by the seasons, the regular ebb and flow of the tide, the coming of light and dark. But it had never before been broken up into artificial units wherein every seventh day was one of refrain from unnecessary labour, no matter how conducive the weather might be to profitable or pleasurable activity. This new regime necessitated new words, and in particular there was a need to define this artificial seven-day period. In Inuktitut, there is a verb, *pinasuaqtuq*, to describe working, being active, or doing something. In Baffin Island and some other parts of the Arctic, the root of this word, with an appropriate affix, *rusiq*, became *pinasuarusiq*—a unit of time measuring activity, therefore a week. (In other parts of the eastern Canadian Arctic, the word is expressed as *sanattailiup akunninga* or *sanattailiit akunningani*.)

Individual days also needed defining. And the most important day for pre-Christian Inuit was not the Sabbath but the day before the Sabbath, for this was the day on which most whalers paid off the Inuit in their employ. Of course, money was an unheard-of commodity in the Arctic. Rather, the whalers paid their assistants in goods, like guns, ammunition, and clothing, and with food items, like tea, coffee, molasses, sugar, and the ever-popular ship's biscuit.

Inuit have a word, *siva*, which Lucien Schneider's dictionary defines as "the solid part of a piece of blubber or fat that was melted over a fire." By analogy, because of its hardness, some Inuit used this word to describe the ship's biscuit that was so popular a food item. One of the joys of Inuktitut, a characteristic that makes it so capable of describing new concepts, is its ability to add an affix or a series of affixes to modify a root word and give it a new or related meaning. In this way, in Baffin Island, *siva* plus *taaq* (an affix showing "getting" or "acquiring") plus *vik* (an affix denoting the time when something occurs) becomes *sivataaqvik*—the time when you get your biscuits. And that day was Saturday.

Today in most Baffin communities, the word *sivataaqvik* still means Saturday. Of course, when one hears the word, no one thinks of biscuits anymore. The word has become lexicalized—it has a new meaning divorced from the sum of its parts. But it was once the most important day of the week—the day when rations were given out. Biscuit Day.

The Mysterious Iisilantimiut

Southern Greenland was colonized over a thousand years ago by Norsemen (and women) from Iceland. Having settled first in the southern fjords of the island, they expanded northwards to establish permanent settlements in the Nuuk area. Extended hunting trips took them even farther north.

In recent decades, Norse artifacts have been found on Baffin Island near Kimmirut and Pond Inlet, and far to the north on an island off the coast of Ellesmere Island.

I've always been interested in the wanderings of these brave Norse refugees from Iceland. And about thirty years ago, I thought, for a brief and exciting time, that I had stumbled upon a linguistic artifact of their presence on Baffin Island.

In the early 1980s, I was researching the story of the killing of Robert Janes by Inuit in north Baffin Island in 1920. The hunter who had shot the Newfoundland trader so many years earlier was Nuqallaq, but he had died in 1925. His young widow, Ataguttiaq, had lived on for another six decades.

I talked with Ataguttiaq, by then a quite elderly woman, in her comfortable home in Pond Inlet. I suppose I was really interviewing her, but my interviews were seldom formal. I rarely used a tape recorder, preferring to take notes during relaxed conversations, punctuated by the requisite numerous cups of tea that were standard fare in Inuit households.

These conversations were more noted for their digressions than for sticking to any particular subject. On the day in question, in response to a comment of mine, Ataguttiaq referred to people she called *Iisilantimiut*. My heart raced. This was a perfect rendition of how an Inuktitut speaker would transform the word *Iceland* into Inuktitut and add the suffix *-miut*, meaning "the people of." Had I stumbled upon a linguistic vestige of an ancient memory of the Greenland Norse, originally from Iceland, and their visits to Baffin Island?

I thought I had, for the reference was to when the Iisilantimiut had come on ships to the Pond Inlet area, staying only for short periods of time. To me, this was of earth-shaking importance, a remembered word that would corroborate the archaeological record!

My excitement lasted about ten minutes. Further questioning revealed that the Iisilantimiut had arrived with the *arvagasuaqtiit* —the bowhead whalers—on Scottish whaling ships. Clearly then, these events had happened in the 1800s, and not six, seven, or more centuries earlier.

But who were these mysterious Iisilantimiut of whom Ataguttiaq spoke? I searched my memory for what I knew of Scottish whalers in High Arctic waters. And then I made the connection.

Scottish whalers referred to the Inuit of Baffin Island in their journals as the Westlanders—the people on the western shores of Davis Strait. If the people of Baffin were the Westlanders, then the Inuit of the Greenland coast must be the Eastlanders. Inuit on Baffin must have learned this word from the whalers and modified it to the sounds of Inuktitut.

Coincidentally, "the people of the Eastland" would be rendered into Inuktitut as *Iisilantimiut*, exactly the same as would "the people of Iceland," the word I thought I had heard.

Indeed, in subsequent readings of whaling literature, I found scattered references to the Eastland and the Eastlanders, and they clearly referred to Greenland and the Inuit who lived there. The word was once common. George Tyson, a whaling captain, wrote in 1878 of the Inuit of Cumberland Sound, "I have had several conversations with the Esquimaux in regard to their going with me to the East Land, as they always call the coast of Greenland."

Occasionally, Scottish whalers picked up Inuit from Greenland communities and took them along as assistants on whaling voyages bound for the Pond Inlet area. Occasionally, Inuit from both sides of Baffin Bay met—Eastlanders and Westlanders. What

Ataguttiaq had told me in casual conversation was a memory she had heard from her parents of one of these encounters, but she had used a very old word, a borrowed English term from the days of the whalers, to describe the Greenlanders. It's a word never heard today—a loan word that served its purpose and has passed out of use and probably, by now, out of memory.

This in itself was an exciting enough discovery for someone interested in language and in the intersection of whaling and Inuit culture. Just not as exciting as if it had been a memory of the ancient Norse in Baffin Island.

Guests of the Whalers

Inuit in New England

Jeannie and Abbott: Inuit Visitors in America

The setting is the same in each picture, indicating that there was only one session. A chair serves as a prop, with the Inuit man leaning against it in one photograph, and the Inuit woman resting an arm on it in another. Furs are draped over the chair for some photographs and laid on the floor for others. A curtain is seen on the left. The Inuit are dressed in skin clothing and both wear *kamiit* (sealskin boots). In another photograph, they are seen together, the woman sitting on a pile of furs, the man seated on the floor, his hand against his cheek, his elbow resting on his wife's knee. The man is tall and thin, a cocky expression on his face. The woman has long hair and a plump face. Both stare directly at the camera. They appear to be in their late twenties.

These are photographs from my personal collection. There are three on stereo cards and one on a glass lantern slide. They are among the very earliest photographs of Canadian Inuit. Ironically, the photographs were not taken in the North but in a photographer's studio in the United States.

Who were these people, and what was their story? Fortunately, there is an answer to both questions.

The stereo cards I acquired are unidentified except for the brief notations on the reverse: "Esquimaux from Baffin's Bay" in the case of the woman, and "Esquimaux Chief, from Baffin's Bay" for the man. The glass slide bears no information. But these images were reproduced in a book, *Narrative of the Second Arctic Expedition Made by Charles F. Hall*, published in 1879. And there was a copy of the man's picture in the Indian and Colonial Research Center in Old Mystic, Connecticut. From these sources we learn their names, and precious little else.

Whalers were notoriously inadequate at pronouncing and writing Inuit names. To make things easier, they usually gave them nicknames in English. Often the Inuit name is recorded, but in an orthography that leaves it unclear how it should be pronounced. This was the case with this couple who visited Groton, Connecticut, in that year.

The man's name is written as Kud-lup-pa-mune, but the whalers called him Abbott. He was a cousin of the famous Ipiirvik, also known as Joe, who was the husband of Tookoolito, whom the whalers called Hannah, the most widely travelled Inuit of their time. (No one is sure what this woman's Inuktitut name really was. Tookoolito was Hall's spelling, but he was notoriously poor at spelling Inuktitut words. In historical records her name is spelled at least ten different ways.)

The woman was Abbott's wife. Her name was recorded as Oo-see-cong; the whalers called her Jeannie.

By the mid-1800s, Inuit were no longer being kidnapped by Qallunaat and taken south, as had happened occasionally in the past. But sometimes a whaling captain would take willing men, or rarely a married couple, back to the United States with him, as a reward for their service. These Inuit volunteered to make such trips.

Captain Sidney O. Budington was one of those whalers who was happy to take Inuit for a holiday in America. Over the years, a number of Inuit from Cumberland Sound and the mouth of Frobisher Bay visited his home on Toll Road in Groton, usually spending a winter with the captain and his obliging family.

In 1866, Budington took Abbott and Jeannie to Groton.

We know nothing of their year with Budington, but we can guess that they were well-treated by the townsfolk, because Budington was a well-respected member of his community. Sidney Budington was forty years old, a veteran whaler. He and his wife, Sarah, had been married for sixteen years. They lived about a mile inland from the ferry that connected Groton to New London, "where a profusion of wild roses grew, in a plain, unpretentious dwelling, painted white, on a hill adjoining a pasture," in the words of Charles Francis Hall. Sarah was four years older than her husband, and had been a schoolteacher. They had two daughters, Victoria and Florence, both in their early teens. Sarah and her children liked having Inuit visitors in their home, and Sarah usually sent gifts back north for their families.

When their vacation with the Budingtons was at an end, Abbott and Jeannie left with the captain on the long journey back to Baffin Island. We don't know the date of their departure, only that it was in late spring. We know this because Jeannie never made it home. She died on the voyage, and the date of her death is recorded on a memorial tombstone in the cemetery at Groton. "Oo-see-cong," it reads, "Died July 1st, 1867. Aged 28 years."

In the absence of any evidence to the contrary, one can assume that Abbott made it safely home to Cumberland Sound.

* * *

The historical record is maddeningly sparse where Inuit are concerned, and nowhere more so than in whaling records. Inuit are introduced, often with indecipherable names, and then often never mentioned again.

This was the case with Abbott. I can find no further reference to him in the meagre writings that exist on whaling in the eastern Arctic.

But a tantalizing shred of information exists that may point to what became of him. During the First International Polar Year, a German scientific party arrived in Cumberland Sound in 1882 to spend a winter near the head of the sound.

They established their station at Sirmilik Bay (the Germans spelled it *Shilmilik*). The location was in a valley about a mile wide, bounded by steep rocky hills; the anchorage was good, and the site was considered ideal. A number of Inuit men worked unloading the ship and assisting with the building construction. They were paid in the currency of the day—bread, coffee, syrup, and plugs of tobacco. But when the *Germania* left on September 7, most of the Inuit left with her, to be dropped off at the Scottish whaling station at Kekerten.

In Those Days

Only one Inuit man, whose name is given as Okkeituk, remained, with his young wife and eighteen-month-old daughter. (It is uncertain whether this man's name would correctly be spelled as *Uqittuq* or *Uqaittuq*, so I will retain the German spelling of *Okkeituk*.) They pitched a caribou-skin tent near the station. Later in the winter, they moved into a snow house. Okkeituk hauled snow or blocks of river ice for water, and did whatever else was necessary to keep the German scientists comfortable. His weekly wage was five pounds of ship's biscuits, a quantity of tea, a cup of syrup, and some tobacco.

Okkeituk had just enough knowledge of English that he could act as interpreter for the scientists when other Inuit came to visit. After freeze-up, the first of those visitors arrived on December 5. The scant historical record left by the scientists notes, "Okkeituk's father-in-law and two other men . . . were travelling with one sledge and a team of 12 dogs. . . . The oldest of the men, Abbok, had worked for the whalers and had visited New York."

Abbok looks like an Inuit name, but it could have been a German mishearing of the name Abbott, by which the man would have identified himself to Qallunaat. The Germans may have thought this was his real name. The information that he had visited New York means that this could well have been the man who travelled south with Budington in 1866, about whom we know so little. Budington is known to have taken other Inuit visitors from Groton to New York, and it is likely that he made the same trip with Abbott.

We will never know for sure if Abbok, whose name appears but once in the historical record, is Abbott, the husband of Jeannie. But it is from scraps such as these that a biography, however deficient, is built.

Inuit Graves in Groton, Connecticut

Abbott (Kud-lup-pa-mune) and Jeannie (Oo-see-cong) were guests of a whaling captain, Sidney O. Budington, and his family in Groton, Connecticut, in the winter of 1866–67. Jeannie died on the return journey north, but Captain Budington saw to it that Jeannie was remembered in Groton. Her name was engraved on a small memorial stone in the Starr Burying Ground there.

In fact, this cemetery contains the graves or memorials of half a dozen Inuit, all of whom had been visitors to the picturesque Connecticut town in the days when whaling was an economic force there and on Baffin Island.

The oldest memorial contains the names of three Inuit. The earliest to die was the unfortunate man whose name is record-ed as Cudlargo. Budington had brought him to Groton in 1859. The following year, Charles Francis Hall, travelling north with Budington, met the Inuk aboard ship; he was returning to Baffin Island from his year of adventure in the south. Hall recorded his name as Kudlago. In fact, it was probably Kallarjuk. Sadly, he did not live to see his homeland again.

On July 1, off the Greenland coast, still three hundred miles from home, Kudlago spoke his last words. Hall recorded the man's pitiful question. "Taku siku? Taku siku?" he asked hope-fully. ("Do you see ice? Do you see ice?") Then the man died. He was thirty-five years old. Budington buried him at sea but had a monument erected in the Starr Burying Ground bearing the man's name, date of death, and age.

In 1862, the already well-travelled Inuit couple Tookoolito and Ipiirvik (Hannah and Joe)—they had been to England in 1853 on a two-year visit—went to the United States with Hall, travelling on

In Those Days

Budington's ship. With them was their infant son, Tarralikitaq—"the butterfly." Tragically, the baby died in New York early in 1863 while he and his parents were on exhibit, providing publicity for Hall's fundraising efforts for his next expedition.

The Budington family arranged the boy's funeral. His name on the grave marker is below that of Cudlargo, and is spelled *Tukilikitak*. His date of death is given as February 28, 1863, and his age as eighteen months.

Oo-see-cong (Jeannie) completes the names of Inuit on this simple marker. Strangely, her date of death was seven years to the day after that of Cudlargo.

Beside this marker stands another Inuit headstone, the story of an expedition chiselled into it in tiny letters. The girl buried here was the adopted child of Tookoolito and Ipiirvik, a sister to Tarralikitaq, the brother she never knew.

Her real name was Isigaittuq, and she had been born in Igloolik. Tookoolito and Ipiirvik adopted her while travelling with Hall on his second expedition. Hall named her Silvia Grinnell Ebierbing (his spelling of Ipiirvik), after the daughter of his patron, Henry Grinnell. Her parents simply called her Panik—"daughter"—which Hall mangled in print as Punna. She and her parents were survivors of a remarkable drift on an ice floe from northern Greenland to just north of Newfoundland. Panik survived the drift, but her health was shattered. Early in 1875, she came down with pneumonia and died on March 18 in Groton.

The letters on the simple headstone tell, in abbreviated form, the life of this much-travelled Inuit girl who died before she was nine. Obscured by the grass at the base of the stone, these words are still faintly visible: "Of such is the Kingdom of Heaven."

Towering over these two headstones is an enormous marker

crowned with the initials "J & H." It is the grave marker for Ipiirvik and Tookoolito, but the marker uses their English names, Joe and Hannah. Tookoolito died in Groton on the last day of December, 1876. She was thirty-eight years old.

The stone has a space, above Tookoolito's details, to record the subsequent death of her husband, whose name is inscribed as Joseph Eberbing (the usual spelling by Qallunaat is Ebierbing). But no date of death is given, and Ipiirvik's body does not lie here. He returned to the Arctic after Tookoolito's death and died on an unknown date in the Kivalliq region.

I've laid flowers at these lonely graves more than once. Others I know from the Arctic have also stood silently in front of them to pay their respects. Three memorials, six Inuit names, but only three bodies, all from the same family. Sidney O. Budington is buried nearby. He and his family ensured that the Inuit who visited Groton in the heyday of whaling would be remembered.

A Reunion: Ipiirvik and Italoo Enoch

Ipiirvik (Joe Ebierbing) and his wife, Tookoolito (Hannah), were among a group of nineteen Inuit and Qallunaat who took to the ice during a fierce storm in October 1872 when it was feared that their ship, the exploration vessel *Polaris,* was about to sink off northern Greenland. The entire party—for all survived the most incredible ice drift in Arctic history—were rescued by the *Tigress* north of Newfoundland the following spring and taken from St. John's to Washington, where they were questioned as part of a government inquiry.

The rest of the crew of the *Polaris,* those who had stayed aboard the ship, had still not been heard from. So the American government sent two relief ships north to search for the missing men. One of the ships was the *Tigress*, the very ship that had rescued the ice-floe party, and which the US government had purchased from her Newfoundland owners.

Her captain for this voyage was James A. Greer. George Tyson, a veteran of the drift on the ice floe, signed on as an officer, and four other survivors joined as crew members. One of them was Ipiirvik, who signed on as interpreter and ordinary seaman using his English name, Joe Ebierbing. Leaving Tookoolito and their daughter behind with friends in Wiscasset, Maine, Ipiirvik boarded the *Tigress* at the Brooklyn Navy Yard on July 14, bound for the Arctic.

After a stop at Disco Bay in Greenland, the *Tigress* steamed north to Smith Sound. On August 14, Captain Greer located the spot in Foulke Fjord where the *Polaris* had spent the previous winter. Using Ipiirvik as an interpreter, Greer learned from an Inuk that the *Polaris* had sunk near that spot, and that its captain, Sidney Budington, and his men had sailed southward in two of the ship's boats. Unknown to Captain Greer, the missing men had been picked up by a Scottish whaler, the *Ravenscraig*, in June, even before the *Tigress* had left New York. With no way of knowing that, Greer turned the *Tigress* towards the Baffin coast in the hope of meeting whalers who might have picked them up or had news of them.

On September 4, the *Tigress* anchored in Naujartalik (the whalers called it Niantilik Harbour), close to the whaling centre of Blacklead Island, in Cumberland Sound. This was Ipiirvik's homeland. He, Tookoolito, and their infant son had left Baffin Island eleven years earlier with Charles Francis Hall aboard the whaler *George Henry*. Now he was seeing friends and relatives for the first time in over a decade. Maddeningly, no account of the *Tigress* voyage describes Ipiirvik's reunion with his countrymen. George Tyson left an account of the voyage that provides only a few snippets of detail—that some of the Inuit whom Hall had met on previous voyages were now at Naujartalik, among them the couple whom the whalers called Bob and Polly, and Polly's half-brother, the old man they called Blind George.

We are left to speculate. The Inuit, many of them closely related to Ipiirvik, would have heard of his travels from New England whalers. They would have inquired about Tookoolito, to whom many of them were also related. They would have asked about the couple's adopted daughter, Panik, whom Hall had purchased for them from an Igloolik family during their five-year trip to Foxe Basin and the Central Arctic. There would have been births, deaths, marriages, even murders to report. And Ipiirvik would have had stories to tell—about life in Groton between expeditions, about the death of Hall, and particularly about the horrendous drift on the ice floe that he had so recently endured.

The *Tigress* remained at Naujartalik for less than two weeks. Too soon, the visit was over. But when the ship weighed anchor on September 16, one extra passenger was on board. Ipiirvik had invited his half-brother, Italoo (probably Ittuluk), to accompany him to Groton to spend the winter. Italoo, who also went by the English name Enoch, thus became one of many Baffin Inuit to spend a winter in New England.

The following summer, Italoo returned north, probably aboard Captain John Spicer's schooner, the *Helen F.* It was a long journey, for they whaled off the Greenland coast first, taking five whales near Cape Farewell. Finally, after ninety-one days, Italoo reached home. Unable to write, he dictated a letter to Ipiirvik and Tookoolito on September 19. It was taken down by another sailor, George Johnson, who brought it back to America. In it, he asks his brother to send him cartridges for his gun and to send letters in care of Captain Spicer's schooner. Italoo must have enjoyed his time in Groton, for he tells Ipiirvik and Tookoolito that he thinks he will stay in the North for two years, "and then I will come home again." But it was not to be. He died in Cumberland Sound later that fall.

FIGURE 1: The *Esquimaux*, a whaling ship from Dundee, Scotland, in the ice off Cape York, Greenland.
SOURCE: KENN HARPER COLLECTION.

FIGURE 2: The *Nova Zembla*, a Dundee whaling ship, is seen here on a calm day near Pond Inlet. She was lost in Dexterity Harbour on the Baffin coast in 1902.
SOURCE: KENN HARPER COLLECTION.

THE "ACTIVE" LEAVING DUNDEE.

FIGURE 3: The *Active*, one of the most successful Arctic whaling ships, leaving Dundee. A crowd of friends, relatives, and well-wishers have come to see the crew off.

SOURCE: FROM *THE ARCTIC WHALERS*, BY BASIL LUBBOCK. GLASGOW: BROWN, SON & FERGUSON, 1937.

FIGURE 4: Captain William Fraser Milne, after whom Milne Inlet near Pond Inlet is named, shot this caribou on Baffin Island.

SOURCE: FROM *THE ARCTIC WHALERS*, BY BASIL LUBBOCK. GLASGOW: BROWN, SON & FERGUSON, 1937.

FIGURE 5: Crew members are busy chopping blubber on the deck of a whaling ship near Pond Inlet.

SOURCE: KENN HARPER COLLECTION.

FIGURE 6: A souvenir ivory knife made by an Inuk for the Scottish whaler and trader Walter Kinnes.

SOURCE: KENN HARPER COLLECTION.

FIGURE 7: Yakki cash. This is a bag made by Inuit for a Shetland whaler. Scottish whalers called Inuit Yakkies. These bags were used for storing tobacco or other small valuables.

SOURCE: SHETLAND MUSEUM AND ARCHIVES, #01075.

FIGURE 8: A crew member prepares rope in preparation for the next sighting of a whale.

SOURCE: KENN HARPER COLLECTION.

FIGURE 9: Loading the flippers and blubber of a bowhead whale in Baffin Bay, before 1902.

SOURCE: KENN HARPER COLLECTION.

FIGURE 10: Baleen, which whalers called whalebone, a valuable product from the mouth of a bowhead whale.

SOURCE: KENN HARPER COLLECTION.

FIGURE 11: In the later days of whaling, whalers hunted walruses and other mammals as well as whales.
Here, walruses are being processed aboard a ship.

SOURCE: KENN HARPER COLLECTION.

FIGURE 12: It was unusual for an Inuit woman to be a hunter, but this woman was. This photo was taken by the Scottish whaleman Captain Milne of a woman who was a crack shot and excellent hunter.

SOURCE: KENN HARPER COLLECTION.

FIGURE 13: Scottish whalers sometimes referred to the Inuit of Baffin Island as the West Coast natives. This group was photographed on a whaling ship in the early 1900s.

SOURCE: KENN HARPER COLLECTION.

FIGURE 14: Sandon Perkins, Arctic photographer, and a scene he shot from the whaling vessel *Morning* in 1906.

SOURCE: KENN HARPER COLLECTION.

FIGURE 15: An excerpt from the log of the whale ship *Aurora* in 1884. The drawing of a whale's tail indicates that a whale was taken on that day.

SOURCE: KENN HARPER COLLECTION.

FIGURE 16: Whaling fiction was popular in the early 1900s. This cover from a popular magazine advertises a whaling adventure story.

FIGURE 17: William Scoresby Junior was a whaler, scientist, author, and inventor. When he retired from whaling, he became a clergyman.

SOURCE: KENN HARPER COLLECTION.

FIGURE 18: Bill Lishman was a sculptor, filmmaker, inventor, and naturalist. Here he is shown on an Arctic cruise ship demonstrating how to start a fire using an ice lens.
SOURCE: COURTESY OF JOHN MACDONALD.

FIGURE 19: Whalers were often trapped in the ice of Davis Strait and Baffin Bay. This sometimes resulted in unexpected winterings, often with tragic consequences.
SOURCE: KENN HARPER COLLECTION.

FIGURE 20: Whalers brought their own musical styles to the Arctic. Inuit learned the accordion from Scottish whalers, playing jigs and reels and adopting Scottish square dances.
SOURCE: GRANGER HISTORICAL PICTURE ARCHIVE / ALAMY STOCK PHOTO.

NIKUJAR, THE BOAT-STEERER AND PILOT.

FIGURE 21: Whalers employed many Inuit men, but it was rare for a woman to have a job other than as a seamstress. This woman, Nikujar, however, worked on the American vessel *George Henry* as a boat-steerer and pilot.

SOURCE: FROM *ARCTIC RESEARCHES AND LIFE AMONG THE ESQUIMAUX*, BY CHARLES FRANCIS HALL. NEW YORK: HARPER & BROTHERS, 1866.

FIGURE 22: Bert Rose, then a teacher at Qikiqtarjuaq (Broughton Island), is seen beside the landmark rock with an inscription carved by whalers at Durban Harbour. SOURCE: COURTESY OF BERT ROSE.

EENOOLOOAPIK.

FIGURE 23: Inuluapik (also spelled Eenoolooapik), a young Inuk from Cumberland Sound, who visited Scotland with the whaler William Penny, in 1839.

SOURCE: FROM *A NARRATIVE OF SOME PASSAGES IN THE HISTORY OF EENOOLOOAPIK: A YOUNG ESQUIMAUX*, BY ALEXANDER M'DONALD. EDINBURGH: FRASER & CO., 1841.

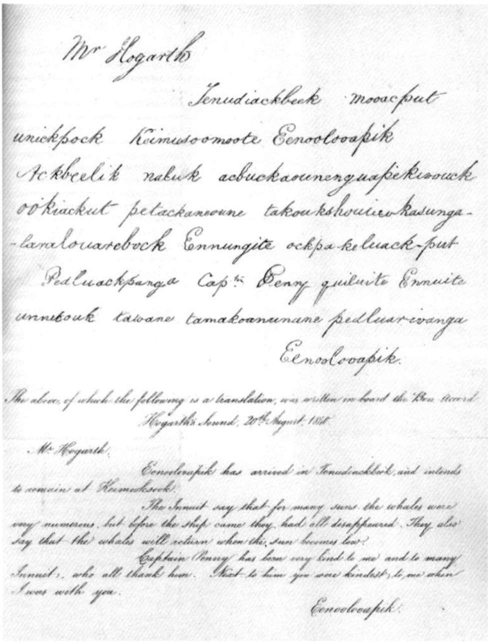

FIGURE 24: Inuluapik met a shipowner, Mr. Hogarth, in Scotland in the winter of 1839–40. On his return to Cumberland Sound, he sent Hogarth this letter.

SOURCE: FROM *A NARRATIVE OF SOME PASSAGES IN THE HISTORY OF EENOOLOOAPIK: A YOUNG ESQUIMAUX*, BY ALEXANDER M'DONALD. EDINBURGH: FRASER & CO., 1841.

FIGURE 25: William Penny was a well-known whaling master from Peterhead, Scotland. With the help of Inuluapik, he found the entrance to Cumberland Sound, not entered by Europeans since the 1500s, and opened it up for whaling.

SOURCE: KENN HARPER COLLECTION.

FIGURE 26: The *Truelove*, one of the most famous Arctic whaling ships, was built in Philadelphia and captured by the British during the American Revolution. She sailed as a whaler from Hull, England, until 1868.

SOURCE: FROM *THE HULL WHALING TRADE*, BY ARTHUR G. CREDLAND. BEVERLEY, EAST YORKSHIRE: THE HUTTON PRESS, 1995.

FIGURE 27: Captain John Parker was for many years the master of the *Truelove*. He rescued the crew of the *McLellan* when that vessel sank in Davis Strait in 1852.

SOURCE: FROM *THE HULL WHALING TRADE*, BY ARTHUR G. CREDLAND. BEVERLEY, EAST YORKSHIRE: THE HUTTON PRESS, 1995.

FIGURE 28: John Kennedy Junior peers out from beneath a famous desk in the Oval Office of the White House while his father, the president, works. The desk is made from timbers of the Arctic exploration ship *Resolute* and was a gift from England to the United States.

SOURCE: PHOTOGRAPHED BY BETTMANN / BETTMANN COLLECTION / GETTY IMAGES, #514079746.

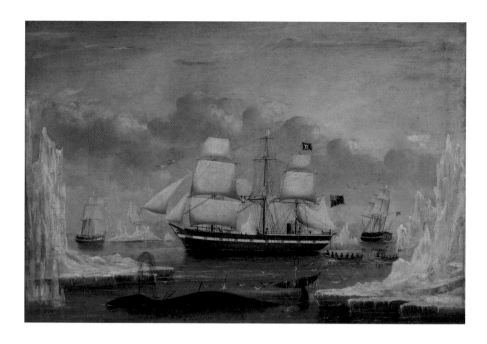

FIGURE 29: The *Diana* was a steam whaler out of Hull, England. She became trapped in the ice of Davis Strait in the fall of 1866. The ship survived the winter, but many of the crew perished.
SOURCE: MARITIME MUSEUM, HULL, UK / BRIDGEMAN IMAGES.

FIGURE 30: Captain John Gravill Senior was master of the whaling ship *Diana* when she was beset by ice in Davis Strait in 1866. He died aboard ship the day after Christmas.
SOURCE: FROM *THE HULL WHALING TRADE*, BY ARTHUR G. CREDLAND. BEVERLEY, EAST YORKSHIRE: THE HUTTON PRESS, 1995.

FIGURE 31: A memorial built in Lerwick, Shetland Islands, to the survivors of the
Diana disaster during the winter of 1866–67.

FIGURE 32: This Inuit woman, Oo-see-cong, known to the whalers as Jeannie, visited Groton, Connecticut, in 1866. She died aboard a whaling ship on her return voyage the following year.
SOURCE: KENN HARPER COLLECTION.

FIGURE 33: Jeannie's husband, Kud-lup-pa-mune, whom the whalers called Abbott, accompanied her to the US and returned to Baffin Island the following year.
SOURCE: KENN HARPER COLLECTION.

FIGURE 34: Jeannie and Abbott were photographed in a studio in the US, and their images were published on stereo cards and glass slides, both popular at the time. SOURCE: KENN HARPER COLLECTION.

FIGURE 35: The names of six Inuit from Baffin Island are remembered on three tombstones in Groton, Connecticut. Only three Inuit bodies are buried there, however.

SOURCE: KENN HARPER COLLECTION.

KUDLAGO.

FIGURE 36: Kudlago, an Inuk from Baffin Island, visited the United States with Captain Sidney O. Budington in the fall of 1859. He died on the journey home the following year.

SOURCE: FROM *ARCTIC RESEARCHES AND LIFE AMONG THE ESQUIMAUX*, BY CHARLES FRANCIS HALL. NEW YORK: HARPER & BROTHERS, 1866.

BURIAL OF KUDLAGO.

FIGURE 37: Kudlago died on the journey north in 1860. He was buried at sea.

SOURCE: FROM *ARCTIC RESEARCHES AND LIFE AMONG THE ESQUIMAUX*, BY CHARLES FRANCIS HALL. NEW YORK: HARPER & BROTHERS, 1866.

FIGURE 38: Scottish whaling captains sometimes took men back to Scotland for a winter, usually as a reward for their service. This man, Urio Etwango, is pictured on a whaling ship in the harbour at Lerwick, Shetland Islands.
SOURCE: SHETLAND MUSEUM AND ARCHIVES, R01265.

FIGURE 39: The *Windward* was a sturdy whaler built in Dundee in 1860 and used by whalers and explorers alike. She sank in 1907 off northern Greenland.
SOURCE: FROM *THE LAST OF THE WHALING CAPTAINS*, BY G. V. CLARK. GLASGOW: BROWN, SON & FERGUSON LTD., 1986.

FIGURE 40: Igarjuaq, the Scottish whaling station near Pond Inlet, in the early 1900s. Canadian Captain Joseph-Elzéar Bernier purchased the station from the Scots.

SOURCE: J. E. BERNIER / LIBRARY AND ARCHIVES CANADA / PA-061522.

FIGURE 41: These Inuit from Pond Inlet visited the whaling ship *Maud* in 1889.

SOURCE: WALTER LIVINGSTONE-LEARMONTH / LIBRARY AND ARCHIVES CANADA / C-088384.

FIGURE 42: James Mutch lost his last ship, the *Vera*, in Sisimiut (Holsteinsborg), Greenland, in 1922. His crew were quartered in the local hospital while they awaited passage to Europe. They called it "Vera Villa" and put up a small sign to that effect that can still be seen today.

SOURCE: KENN HARPER COLECTION.

FIGURE 43: Nivissannaq, known to whalers as Shoofly after a popular American song, was the local "wife" of whaling captain George Comer.

SOURCE: FROM *REPORT OF THE DOMINION GOVERNMENT EXPEDITION TO HUDSON BAY AND THE ARCTIC ISLANDS ON BOARD THE D. G. S. NEPTUNE 1903–04*, BY A. P. LOW. OTTAWA: GOVERNMENT PRINTING BUREAU, 1906.

FIGURE 44: Inuit visitors were always welcome on Comer's ship. Here, a group of women in beaded dress are posed for a photograph at Fullerton.

SOURCE: FROM *REPORT OF THE DOMINION GOVERNMENT EXPEDITION TO HUDSON BAY AND THE ARCTIC ISLANDS ON BOARD THE D. G. S. NEPTUNE 1903–04*, BY A. P. LOW. OTTAWA: GOVERNMENT PRINTING BUREAU, 1906.

FIGURE 45: Ippaktuq, also known as Tasseok—Harry to the whalers—was an Aivilingmiut man and leader of the Inuit who were working for Comer.

SOURCE: FROM *REPORT OF THE DOMINION GOVERNMENT EXPEDITION TO HUDSON BAY AND THE ARCTIC ISLANDS ON BOARD THE D. G. S. NEPTUNE 1903–04*, BY A. P. LOW. OTTAWA: GOVERNMENT PRINTING BUREAU, 1906.

FIGURE 46: George Comer, whom the Inuit called Angakkuq (the shaman), earned his nickname because of his ability as a photographer. He developed his pictures aboard ship, and the results impressed local Inuit.

FIGURE 47: Trypots, in which oil was separated from blubber, lie abandoned at the former whaling station of Blacklead Island in Cumberland Sound.

SOURCE: KENN HARPER COLLECTION.

FIGURE 48: All that remains of the grave of a whaler from Peterhead who was buried over a century ago on Cemetery Island in Cumberland Sound, near the Blacklead Island whaling station.

SOURCE: KENN HARPER COLLECTION.

FIGURE 49: The Blacklead Island whaling station in 1903, near the end of the whaling era.

FIGURE 50: Inuit on board the *Diana* at Blacklead Island in 1897.

FIGURE 51: Casks being rolled to the beach for loading onto the whaling vessel *Thomas*, Blacklead Island, 1911.

SOURCE: KENN HARPER COLLECTION.

FIGURE 52: Alexander Murray Senior was an experienced whaling master. Both his sons, John and Alexander Junior, followed in his footsteps and became captains of whale ships. They are well-remembered by Inuit in Baffin Island and Repulse Bay.

SOURCE: FROM *THE LAST OF THE WHALING CAPTAINS*, BY G. V. CLARK. GLASGOW: BROWN, SON & FERGUSON LTD., 1986.

FIGURE 53: Alexander Murray Senior was awarded the British Government's Arctic Medal for his service in the search for the missing expedition led by Sir John Franklin. The inscription reads, "For Arctic Discoveries. 1818–1855."
SOURCE: KENN HARPER COLLECTION.

FIGURE 54: Austin Murray was the son of Captain John Murray. He remembered a famous whaling song, "The Dead Horse Song." The author visited him in his home near Dundee in 2003.
SOURCE: KENN HARPER COLLECTION.

FIGURE 55: David Cardno, from Peterhead, Scotland, made his first trip to the Arctic at age thirteen. He later spent many years as a whaler and trader in Cumberland Sound.

SOURCE: ILLUSTRATED BY DIANNE SUTHERLAND / *A WHALER'S TALE: THE MEMOIRS OF DAVID HAWTHORN CARDNO OF PETERHEAD 1853–1938*, EDITED BY GAVIN SUTHERLAND. ABERDEEN: ABERDEENSHIRE COUNCIL, DEPT. OF LEISURE AND RECREATION, 1996.

FIGURE 56: George Cleveland was an American whaler turned trader in the Repulse Bay area. Inuit called him Sakkuartirungniq—"the harpooner."

SOURCE: DANISH ARCTIC INSTITUTE / THERKEL MATHIASSEN.

FIGURE 57: George Cleveland had children by a number of Inuit women. Many Nunavummiut today trace their ancestry to this ribald, eccentric man.

SOURCE: FROM "REPORT ON THE EXPEDITION," BY THERKEL MATHIASSEN, IN *REPORT OF THE FIFTH THULE EXPEDITION 1921–24*, VOL. 1, NO. 1. COPENHAGEN: GYLDENDALSKE BOGHANDEL, 1946.

FIGURE 58: William Duval was a German-born American whaler who went to the Arctic as a young man and married an Inuit woman and raised a family in the Arctic. He spent most of his life in Cumberland Sound, dying there in 1931.
SOURCE: KENN HARPER COLLECTION.

FIGURE 59: William Duval is pictured here with his wife and two daughters and an unidentified young man outside his home at Usualuk in Cumberland Sound.
SOURCE: SCOTT POLAR RESEARCH INSTITUTE, UNIVERSITY OF CAMBRIDGE, WITH PERMISSION.

FIGURE 60: Jack Taylor was the captain of the *Easonian*, one of the last of the Scottish whaling and trading ships in Baffin Island. It sank at Kekerten in 1922.

SOURCE: KENN HARPER COLLECTION.

FIGURE 61: A whale ship in the ice off the Baffin coast, before 1902.
SOURCE: KENN HARPER COLLECTION.

FIGURE 62: The *Albert* was a ship well-known to Inuit. Built in 1889, she sank in Davis Strait in 1968.
SOURCE: KENN HARPER COLLECTION.

FIGURE 63: A veteran harpooner beside a harpoon gun in Baffin Bay, before 1902.
SOURCE: KENN HARPER COLLECTION.

FIGURE 64:
A whaler at Blacklead Island displays baleen marked for shipment to a trading company.
SOURCE: KENN HARPER COLLECTION.

FIGURE 65: American whalers caught in the ice of Melville Bay in 1852.
SOURCE: KENN HARPER COLLECTION.

A Literary Icon in the Arctic

Arthur Conan Doyle

Arthur Conan Doyle is one of the most well-known writers in English literature, famous for his creation of the detective Sherlock Holmes. Born in Edinburgh, Scotland, in 1859, he studied medicine in that city from the age of seventeen to twenty-two. But in early 1880, he interrupted his studies for a journey to the Arctic as medical officer aboard a Peterhead-based whaler, the *Hope*, under the veteran captain John Gray.

Conan Doyle went on to establish a medical practice and make a name for himself as a writer, known for a large number of works, not only his crime fiction so well remembered today in the Sherlock Holmes stories. One of the most popular authors of modern times, he was also a sportsman, a crusader for social and criminal justice, a war correspondent, and a military historian.

In Those Days

In 1880, Holmes recorded his time aboard the *Hope* in two letters that he sent home to his mother, Mary, and in a hand-illustrated diary. As well as attending to sick crew members, he took an active part in sealing and whaling. In those times, as Arctic whaling was in decline, sealing often preceded the actual whaling. The young man turned twenty-one years of age at 80° north latitude.

The first letter home was written from Lerwick in Shetland, where vessels routinely stopped to hire the remainder of their crews and to wait out the time before it was reasonable to head farther north. There was no point in reaching the sealing grounds too early, as an Act of Parliament prevented the killing of a seal before April 2.

He wasn't impressed with Lerwick, describing it as "the town of crooked streets, and ugly maidens, and fish. A most dismal hole, with 2 hotels & 1 billiard table. Country round is barren & ugly. No trees in the island."

But he liked his fellow seamen, whom he characterized as "fine honest fellows" and "such a strapping lot." He was astonished at how informed and self-educated some of them were, writing, "The chief engineer came up from the coal hole last night & engaged me upon Darwinism, in the moonlight on deck. . . . The captain is a well informed man too."

There were thirty whale ships waiting at Lerwick while Conan Doyle was there. Only two of them, the *Hope* and the *Windward*, were from Peterhead, and rivalry ran strong between their crews and those from the rival Scottish port, Dundee. Conan Doyle recorded a barroom brawl in which the *Hope*'s first mate, Colin McLean, tired of hearing his ship denigrated, wreaked havoc on half a dozen Dundee officers. "He floored a doctor & maimed a captain & got away in triumph," wrote Doyle. "He remarked to me in the morning, 'It's lucky I was sober, Doctor, or there might have been a row.' I wonder what Colin's idea of a row might be."

His second letter home was written on April 7, from 73° north latitude, after sealing had commenced. They had left Shetland on March 10 and by March 20 had reached ice laden with basking seals. "They were lying in a solid mass upon the ice," he wrote, "about 15 miles by 8, literally millions of them. On the 22nd we got upon the edge of them and waited. 25 vessels were in sight doing the same thing." But still they had to wait until the season opened, and in the meantime a gale arose on March 29, breaking up the pack and dispersing the seals. When hunting finally opened, the results were poor.

He wrote about this first experience of sealing: "On the 3rd the bloody work began and it has been going on ever since. The mothers are shot and the little ones have their brains knocked out with spiked clubs. They are then skinned where they lie and the skin with blubber attached is dragged by the assassin to the ship's side. This is very hard work, as you often have to travel a couple of miles, as I did today, jumping from piece to piece before you find your victim, and then you have a fearful weight to drag back."

They were off Jan Mayen Island and here Conan Doyle was exhilarated, despite falling into the water five times in the first four days, earning himself the nickname "Great Northern Diver." He frightened his poor mother with a description of his first tumble into the frigid water: "The first time I tried to get on to the ice, there was a fine strong piece alongside, and I was swinging myself down on to it by a rope, when the ship gave a turn of her propeller sending me clear of the ice and into the sea with 28° of frost on. I was hauled out by a boat hook in my coat, and went on the ice again when I had changed, without mishap." The following day he fell in three more times. His diary told a hair-raising story about one of these falls, one in which he could very easily have lost his life: "I just killed a seal on a large piece [of ice] when I fell over the side. Nobody was near and the water was deadly cold. I had hold of the edge of the ice to prevent my sinking, but it was too smooth and slippery to climb up by, but at last I got hold of the seal's hind flippers and managed to pull myself up by them."

With the young sealing finished, the *Hope* steamed for Spitzbergen and the long-awaited whaling. Unfortunately, no letters resulted from that part of the adventure.

* * *

The adventurous life aboard ship agreed with Conan Doyle. From Lerwick he had written to his mother that "you will be glad to hear that I never was more happy in my life. I've got a strong Bohemian element in me, I'm afraid, and the life just seems to suit me." In his later letter from the High Arctic, he wrote, "I never before knew what it was like to be thoroughly healthy," adding, "I just feel as if I could go anywhere or do anything." When the *Hope* returned to Scotland on August 10, he noted symptoms of withdrawal in his diary: "The green grass on shore looks very cool and refreshing to me after nearly 6 months never seeing it, but the houses look revolting. I hate the vulgar hum of men and would like to be back at the floes again."

He never did return to the Arctic, although he spent one spell as ship's doctor off the African coast. But he maintained a lifelong interest in the North. In 1882, he sold a story, "The Captain of the Pole-Star," to *Temple Bar* magazine for ten guineas. It drew upon his Arctic adventures aboard the *Hope* and appeared in

January of the following year. That it was in part autobiographical is evidenced by the subtitle, "Being an extract from the singular journal of John M'Alister Ray, student of medicine," although the lunatic master of the title, Captain Nicholas Craigie, bore no resemblance to the kindly Captain Gray of the *Hope*.

In 1883, Conan Doyle gave a lecture on "The Arctic Seas" to the Portsmouth Literary & Scientific Society, which was "an unqualified and splendid success." The lecture also gave him "a quite unmerited reputation as a sportsman, for," he wrote, "I borrowed from a local taxidermist every bird and beast he possessed which could conceivably find its way into the Arctic Circle. These I piled upon the lecture table, and the audience, concluding that I had shot them all, looked upon me with great respect. Next morning they were back with the taxidermist once more."

In 1884, he submitted an article, "Modern Arctic Discovery," to *Good Words* magazine, but there is no indication that it was published.

When Norwegian explorer Fridtjof Nansen lectured at London's Albert Hall on February 8, 1897, Conan Doyle was in attendance. And he attended a luncheon in honour of Robert Peary in May 1910. He poked good-natured fun at the great explorer's accomplishments. "Writers of romance had always a certain amount of grievance against explorers," he said. "There had been a time when the world was full of blank spaces, and in which a man of imagination might be able to give free scope to his fancy. But owing to the ill-directed energy of their guest and other gentlemen of similar tendencies these spaces were rapidly being filled up; and the question was where the romance writer was to turn." Ten years later, he met another Arctic explorer, Vilhjalmur Stefansson, whom he described as "a dear fellow and a hero."

In Those Days

Arthur Conan Doyle was knighted in 1902. He died on July 7, 1930, beloved by his countrymen and admired by Sherlock Holmes fans worldwide. The epitaph on his grave marker reads, "Steel True. Blade Straight," and describes him as "Knight, Patriot, Physician & Man of Letters."

The *Windward*

A Sturdy Arctic Ship

A Whaling Ship
in the Service of Explorers

The *Windward* was built in 1860 at Stephens and Forbes yard in the port of Peterhead, designed as a sailing whale ship, a three-masted barque of 321 gross tons. But the days of sailing vessels in the whaling fleet were almost over, and the little vessel was fitted with engines in 1866.

She had a reasonably successful career out of Peterhead, travelling often to the northern waters of Davis Strait but also to the sea off the east coast of Greenland. In 1893, her last year sailing from Peterhead, she was under the command of a veteran, Captain David Gray; she took only one whale, which yielded nineteen tons of oil. But the profitability of whaling was declining, and her owners sold her early the following year to Captain Joseph

Wiggins, who in turn sold her the same year to Alfred Harmsworth, a wealthy newspaper owner, who had been searching for a vessel for the use of Frederick George Jackson on an Arctic adventure known as the Jackson-Harmsworth expedition.

That year, the *Windward* took the expedition to Franz Josef Land, which they reached on September 8. Jackson constructed his winter camp there—inexplicably named Elmwood. Ice prevented the *Windward*'s departure, and the sturdy vessel wintered nearby.

Jackson wanted to delineate the islands that made up Franz Josef Land because he had thought they were part of a larger land mass, perhaps extending to the pole. As he found out, this was not the case. He conducted his exploration over the next three years by small boat, dogs and sledges, and ponies. In the meantime, the *Windward*, free of the ice by July 3, 1895, left for London. The following summer, she was back in late July with supplies for the expedition. When she departed on August 7, she carried an unexpected passenger, the Norwegian explorer Fridtjof Nansen, who had wintered even farther north. Nansen had set out in 1893 aboard the *Fram*, which he had frozen into the polar pack to test his theories about ice drift. With one companion, he attempted unsuccessfully to reach the North Pole over the ice. They wintered north of Jackson's expedition, unaware of its existence, and thinking themselves to be near Svalbard. Amazingly, they stumbled upon Jackson's camp and learned their true location. Captain Brown of the *Windward* safely delivered Nansen to Tromso, Norway, in August 1896.

The next summer, the *Windward* arrived on July 22 to pick up the entire expedition. Two weeks later, it left for home.

Harmsworth was finished with the trusty vessel and offered her to Robert Peary for his own attempts to reach the North Pole. In 1898, Captain Samuel Bartlett took command of the ship and sailed for northern Greenland with supplies for Peary, who had travelled ahead on the *Hope*. Picking Peary up at Etah, the *Windward* attempted to force her way farther north but was stopped by ice a little more than halfway up the Ellesmere Island coast, where the vessel wintered at Cape D'Urville. In late August, she left for the south, leaving Peary at Etah.

The next year, Captain Bartlett brought the ship north again with supplies for the American expedition. The plan was to return south that same summer. On board were two visitors whom Peary was not expecting—his wife, Josephine, and young daughter, Marie. But ice stopped the ship and it was forced to winter at Payer Harbour, again on the Canadian side of Smith Sound. Peary, not expecting a visit from his wife, and not knowing for some months where the ship was, did not travel to the *Windward* until the following May. When the ship was free of ice and headed south that summer, it was with Mrs. Peary and her daughter but without Robert, who would spend one more year in northern Greenland.

Peary had no further use for the ship, and she went back into service a few years later as a whaler.

The Wreck of the *Windward*

By 1904, the *Windward* was back at work as a whaler. She had been out of the trade for some years. The Dundee firm of R. Ferguson and Company purchased her to replace their ship, the *Vega*, which had been crushed in the ice of Melville Bay. Her first year was not a particular success—she took only one young whale, which yielded a mere seven feet of bone.

In Those Days

In 1906, the *Windward*, under Captain Cooney, was the last ship home, and she arrived clean. For almost three months, she had been beset by ice in the treacherous waters of Melville Bay. Finally clear at the end of July, she made for Cape Hooper on the Baffin coast. Although she took no whales, she did return home with fifty-four walruses, thirteen seals, thirteen bearskins, two live bears, four narwhals, and one beluga. It was a common occurrence in the dying days of whaling for whalers to take walrus and seal. Bearskins were valuable, but a live bear brought a much larger sum when it was sold to a zoo. And whalers traded regularly for skins and ivory with Inuit whom they met on the Baffin coast. Veteran whalers referred to all these non-whale products as "scraps."

The following year, the *Windward* was off to a good start. Early out of Dundee, by June 14 she had made a quick and uneventful crossing of Melville Bay. But, perhaps as a portent of things to come, the engineer, forty-two-year-old Donald Wilson, died that day. Eleven days later, off the Carey Islands, a group of over a dozen small islands near the coast of northern Greenland, the ship hit a submerged rock. Unfortunately, the accident happened at high tide. When the tide ebbed, the vessel listed, slipped, and was badly holed near the stern. Water rushed in, and the pumps could not keep up. The crew took to the ship's six boats and loaded them with provisions—tinned beef, margarine, coffee, tea, condensed milk, vegetables, sardines, ham, and biscuits, as well as one hundred pounds of coal.

After a night camped on one of the islands, the decision was made to row to Pond's Bay, the whalers' name for the waters around present-day Pond Inlet. They knew there was a shore-based Dundee station there, and there would be other whaling ships calling.

They left at 8:00 A.M. on June 27, in front of a northeast breeze, each crew member well clad and with a blanket. James Henderson, the carpenter, kept a private log of the adventure.

They set a course for Clarence Head on Ellesmere Island, about thirty-five miles distant. But Henderson soon lost sight of the other boats. Late in the afternoon, after cooking a meal on a floating pan of ice, they adjusted their course for Coburg Island at the mouth of Glacier Strait. There was a light wind from the north, so progress was good. The crew lay down to rest as Henderson continued to steer using an oar, the boat being propelled by wind. But as they neared their landmark, they saw that ice sixteen to twenty feet thick closed the mouth of the strait. They kept the boats well off this barrier, for safety, and steered south.

Late on the morning of June 29, they pulled the boat onto the ice and the carpenter fashioned a rudder from some wood they were carrying. It would make steering considerably easier. The next day, they set a course to cross the strait to Devon Island. The crew complained of swollen feet and ankles, chapped lips, and frozen noses. The crossing, though, was successful, and the reward was a square meal of bread, beef, and curry.

They had travelled with little or no sleep. Henderson wrote in his log, "I am done up for the want of sleep. I have not had any since the morning we lost the ship. I have been so long without it that I cannot fall over. My mind is wandering at times. The younger ones seem to sleep all right sitting in their boats with their blankets over them, but the anxiety of my mind keeps me from it."

In Those Days

A Bittersweet Rescue and Homecoming

Halfway down the western coast of Devon Island, Henderson saw the other five boats approaching. On July 1, at 8:00 A.M., this "flotilla" left for Cape Hay at the northeastern tip of Bylot Island, with a northeast wind helping their passage. But the wind died in midafternoon, and the crew took once again to the oars. By eight in the evening, they faced a stiff headwind and snow squalls, and the floating ice pans proved a constant danger.

The next day, with the wind still blowing from the southwest, they launched the boats in the evening. Henderson wrote:

> [We] were about to get away when a large piece of ice came in, unnoticed by any of us, jammed the boats' head, and walked right over us, filling us right up with water. I thought it was to be the last of us, and all we had for a home. The ice eased off and she floated flush with the surface of the water. Thank God for it. I never thought she would right with the water that was in her. We got her partly hauled up on the ice again, and bailed out. Everything was soaked, our bread was damaged, and nothing was dry except what was on our backs. It was hard looking at our wrecked home. We got the water out, and examined her, and found that our rudder was broken beyond repair. Proceeded to load up again . . . and launched the boat, set sail, and ran north-west with two reefs in our sail—four boats of us towards the land in blinding sleet.[1]

On July 3, heavy masses of ice threatened again to sink the boats. The carpenter wrote:

---

[1] Anonymous, "Adrift in the Arctic Seas," *People's Journal* (November 16, 1907).

It was a case of down sail quick and pull hard head on to the wind; a pull for dear life to windward. Otherwise we would have been smashed up to matchwood. It was blowing a strong gale from the north-east. About 4 P.M. the gale moderated, but a swell came in and broke up the flow [*sic*] on which we had taken refuge, threatening to swallow us up, boats and all. The three of us—the captain's, mate's, and my boat—were together. We made preparations to try to save one of the boats and some provisions for the 20 men in them. We hauled the boats over the tops of high pinnacles of ice till sometimes they were only bearing in the centre and sometimes standing on one end. We worked hard cutting pieces off the hummocks with axes in order to get the boats to a place of safety. [2]

But the swell subsided. By 2:00 A.M. on July 6, they were only ten miles from the station at Pond's Bay. They pulled their boats onto a floe and slept for four hours. At nine in the morning, they were spotted by the Dundee ship *Morning*, which picked up the three boats' crews, then steamed north to rescue the others.

The crew were divided up among the *Morning*, the *Eclipse*, and the *Balaena*. All these ships returned to Dundee clean, a disaster for the owners. One of the shipwrecked crew, Hans Neilsen, a Swede, died aboard the *Eclipse*, from the ordeal he had experienced before their rescue.

It was a bittersweet homecoming. They were safe, but because of the peculiarities of how whalers were paid, they were also broke, with "not a single copper to draw on their arrival." By tradition, crew members received one month's wages in advance

---

[2]Anonymous, "Adrift in the Arctic Seas."

In Those Days

before they left on a voyage. While away, their relatives were able to draw half pay. But when news of the loss of the *Windward* reached Dundee in October, the half pay stopped. The cruel reality was that the *Windward* went down on June 25, and it was on that day that the crew was deemed to have stopped earning wages. In fact, the money drawn by their families between June 25 and the day the news reached Dundee was money that the crew were not entitled to. It instantly became a debt owing to the shipowners. The men had lost everything except the clothes they returned in. For tradesmen who had lost their tools as well, it was an even greater tragedy.

The *Windward* was insured, its shareholders protected. The ship, fifty-seven years old, a ripe old age by whaling standards, lay in the waters off the Carey Islands, one less vessel in the declining Dundee fleet.

James Mutch

An Arctic Whaleman

Mutch, the Legendary Whaler

When I moved north and learned Inuktitut, I began to hear elders
speak of a legendary Qallunaaq who had been an important figure in the whaling days on the east coast of Baffin Island. Most
whalers of the time were given Inuktitut names—like Sivutiksaq
(William Duval) or Angakkuq (George Comer). But this man's
name was Jiimi Maatsi, an obvious English name rendered into
Inuktitut. Still, it took me a while to realize that his real name
was Jimmy (really James) Mutch. Everywhere I lived—Arctic Bay,
Pangnirtung, Padloping Island, Qikiqtarjuaq, and Iqaluit—older
people remembered him. In Pond Inlet and Clyde River, too, his
memory was strong.

111

In Those Days

Over the years, I determined to learn as much as I could about this mysterious man whose career in Baffin had spanned so many years. It wasn't easy, and, to this day, I've never seen a picture of him.

James Shepherd Mutch was born in Boddam, near Peterhead, Scotland, on December 15, 1847. Coming from a poor family, he never had a chance to go to school. Nevertheless, he learned to read and write—he was a self-educated man. As luck would have it, he became a servant in the home of Crawford Noble of Aberdeen, owner of a whaling company that sent ships to the Arctic.

At the age of eighteen, James Mutch sailed to the High Arctic as third mate aboard the *Queen*, a vessel whose home port was Peterhead. The vessel wintered off the coast of Devon Island, giving Mutch his first taste of the far North through the dark season. On the way home the following September, it put in briefly at Naujartalik, a whaling centre in Cumberland Sound.

In 1867, Mutch returned to Cumberland Sound, working again for Crawford Noble. Eventually he took over the management of Noble's Kekerten whaling station. He was still there in 1883 when a German scientist, Franz Boas, arrived in Cumberland Sound for a year of study.

In 1885, James Mutch returned to Scotland for a year. While there, he married. He and his wife, Jessie, would have only one child, a girl, Jeannie, born in December 1887.

After his marriage, Mutch continued to work in the Arctic. While there, and despite his marriage, he had relationships with Inuit women, as did many whalers. He returned to Peterhead more often than before, but his career in the Arctic was far from over. Usually he was in Cumberland Sound, sometimes at Kekerten, sometimes at Blacklead Island on the opposite coast.

Collected Writings on Arctic History

The Whaler and the Anthropologist

When the young anthropologist Franz Boas arrived in Cumberland Sound for a year of research in 1883, he was fortunate in having a letter of introduction to James Mutch from Crawford Noble. Mutch agreed to help the anthropologist and his servant, Wilhelm Weike, and opened up his small home at Kekerten to them. The research that Boas conducted in Cumberland Sound formed the basis for his classic work *The Central Eskimo*.

The winter that Boas spent living at Kekerten, often in Mutch's house, was Mutch's seventeenth winter in the Arctic; he knew the Inuit intimately and spoke their language fluently. (Despite this impressive number of winterings, Mutch had visited Scotland occasionally. It was sometimes possible to travel home in the spring on a ship that wintered and return to the Arctic in the fall to winter again.) Without the assistance of Mutch, it is doubtful if Boas would have learned a lot of the information that he did in less than a year among the Inuit. Let's look at some of the evidence to support this statement.

On September 4, 1883, Boas wrote a letter to his fiancée in Germany telling about the events immediately after his arrival: "After I showed Mr. Mutch . . . the letter from Mr. Noble . . . he was very kind and promised to be helpful in every way. My belongings were to be brought on land the next day. In the evening we visited all the topics (Eskimo tents)."

Boas acknowledged his indebtedness to Mutch. In another letter to his fiancée, written after he had been at Kekerten for only three months, he wrote, "Mutch is in every way obliging towards me and helps me with his better knowledge of the Eskimo language wherever he can, so I am greatly indebted to him for increasing my knowledge in this regard. Also he has been lending me his dogs for excursions; in short I must be grateful to him in every way."

Later he wrote, "He has learned much in this country and is an open, honourable character, who moreover does not attempt to conceal his weaknesses." The weaknesses to which Boas referred were Mutch's relationship with at least one Inuit woman and the existence of a young daughter, Analukulu, whom Boas met on a sled trip in the sound.

When Boas began to study the Inuit culture in detail, he acknowledged Mutch's unstinting assistance with these words: "Now I began in earnest to make my ethnographical studies, and was greatly helped by Mr. Mutch."

Boas was hampered in his studies by his poor understanding of English. Most of the Inuit, especially the men, spoke some English, having learned it from both Scottish and American whalers. But Mutch's English was difficult for Boas to understand, for it was a unique dialect of Scots called Doric, spoken in and around Peterhead. "The English I am learning here is worse than atrocious," he wrote. "I'm afraid it is more Scottish than English." And it wasn't just English that Boas had trouble with. Learning Inuktitut was critical to his success, yet in December he wrote, "Now the Eskimos are sitting around me here, telling each other old stories. What a pity that I cannot understand any of it." A week later he wrote, "Gradually I can make myself understood somewhat with the Eskimos. Their language is horribly difficult!"

Boas never returned to the Arctic after he left in 1884. But the following year, he began a remarkable correspondence with Mutch, a series of exchanges that lasted for over thirty years. (He also corresponded with the whaler George Comer and the missionary Edmund Peck.) Mutch's letters were chatty, sometimes gossipy, and filled with information about whaling, hunting, and the lives of the Inuit.

At Boas's instigation, Mutch also collected legends and objects of Inuit material culture. He made a major collection in Cumberland Sound between 1897 and 1899, which enabled Boas to publish the first volume of a two-volume set in 1901, under the title of *The Eskimo of Baffin Land and Hudson Bay*. Although Comer contributed to the work, the vast majority of the information came from James Mutch. He contributed seventy-two of the eighty-one legends and stories in the section "Tales from Cumberland Sound." Boas gave him his due when he wrote, "Ever since that time [1883] Captain Mutch has manifested a keen interest in Eskimo ethnology. . . . From time to time he has sent me valuable replies to inquiries regarding obscure points. . . . In the fall of 1899 Captain Mutch sent to the Museum his collection and the notes which are embodied in the present paper."

Between 1900 and 1902, he collected more material from Cumberland Sound for Boas, and between 1903 and 1908 collected information and objects near present-day Pond Inlet.

James Mutch was unschooled but not uneducated. His assistance over the years was invaluable to Boas, whose career in anthropology had its beginnings with the assistance of Mutch as host, benefactor, and interpreter. Boas described Mutch as "a remarkably good collector" who "obtains with his specimens the fullest information." In his own right, Mutch was a rough and untutored ethnographer, living among the Inuit for over half a century in conditions ideal for the role he voluntarily assumed as collector for Boas.

In Those Days

Trading at Pond's Bay

In 1902, a Scottish shipowner, J. M. M. Mitchell, established the Dundee Pond's Bay Company and purchased a sturdy little vessel, the *Albert*. She—it's peculiar that ships are called "she" even when they have names like *Albert*—had been built in 1890 at Fellows' Yard in Great Yarmouth as a hospital ship for the Royal National Mission to Deep Sea Fishermen. A sailing vessel 101 feet long, with tonnage of 155 gross and 89 net, she was built of oak with a teak deck. The phrases "Heal the Sick" and "Preach the Word" were inscribed on her bows, and the text "Follow me, and I will make you fishers of men" graced her wheel.

By 1903, James Mutch had worked for Crawford Noble, the whaling entrepreneur from Aberdeen, for decades. But in that year, he resigned his position and joined Mitchell's fledgling enterprise. Mitchell had wanted him in his employ, for Mutch knew the North and the whaling trade. He also knew the Inuit and their language. For Mitchell, Mutch launched a new venture, a whaling voyage to northern Baffin Island, which, unlike Cumberland Sound, had never had a permanent whaling presence before.

In 1903, Mutch sailed the *Albert* from Dundee to Pond's Bay. He intended to keep the vessel permanently in the Arctic at a harbour there. The ship would in effect become a floating but anchored whaling and trading station. White whales and narwhals would be hunted from smaller boats, and Inuit would hunt whales on their own or as agents of Mitchell's company. Mutch would also trade with the natives.

But on the way to Pond's Bay, Mutch took the *Albert* first to Cumberland Sound, where he hired a number of Inuit and one white man willing to relocate with him to northern Baffin Island.

The white man was another veteran whaler, William Duval. Known to the Inuit as Sivutiksaq, Duval had lived for over two decades in Cumberland Sound, where he worked for a number of whaling companies, was married after native fashion to an Inuit woman, and spoke the Inuit language fluently. His home was usually at Blacklead Island, a popular shore station in the sound and, since 1894, a Christian mission. Duval's influence was instrumental in convincing two boats' crews of experienced Inuit whalers from Blacklead to move with their families far to the north. Duval was accompanied by his wife, Aulaqiaq, their two daughters, Tauki and Aluki, their two sons, Natsiapik and Qakulluk, and Duval's older son by another woman, Killaq.

Thirty years ago, elderly Inuit remembered the names of some of the brave Inuit who were willing to travel farther north than they had ever been to help Mutch in his whaling enterprise. Some of the names remembered were Suqqulaaq, Kuki, Tautuarjuq, and Agjalik. But perhaps the most important ones were Kanaaka, a natural leader of his people and a man who went on to become a trader in his own right, and Viivi (Veevee), a man of equal stature and respect who happened to be Duval's brother-in-law.

The *Albert* passed its first winter in the High Arctic at Erik Harbour, well to the east of present-day Pond Inlet, but Mutch experienced poor whaling there the following spring. With the summer thaw, he sailed the ship north and west into Admiralty Inlet, where he left Duval and his family to winter and to assess the whaling and trading possibilities there.

The *Albert* returned to Pond's Bay, entering the small strait between Beloeil Island and the Baffin mainland, offshore from the place the Inuit called Igarjuaq, "the big cooking-place," so called because it resembled a hearth, especially when the wind-driven fog moved out from the harbour like smoke from between the boulders. The Inuit called the harbour Tuqsukattak, but Mutch named it Albert Harbour, after his ship. He and his Cumberland Sound Inuit established their shore station, the first permanent trading station in the High Arctic, near a camp of Tununirmiut on the mainland just west of the harbour, near Igarjuaq. He also built a storehouse on the northern shore of Pond's Bay at Button Point on Bylot Island.

Mutch thought the Inuit of Pond's Bay drove a hard bargain, their skills no doubt learned through decades of dealing with Scottish whalers during the brief High Arctic summers. "The real Pond's Bay Eskimo," he wrote, "had been coming and going all winter, trading a fox-skin when they had one, but always wanting nearly the home value for it for anything they might bring. They had an idea that sealskins were worth more than ten times what they were sold for in the London market. . . . When a bear-skin was brought, though it was small, a telescope or a gun was asked for it."

Winters were hard for the Pond's Bay Inuit, and Mutch attributed this to the paucity of sled dogs. "Without dogs," he noted, "they cannot all get to the best hunting-ground, and even at the best ones, I can hardly say that I have seen thus far, nor have I heard of, any good catches of seals." He thought many of the men were reliable and conscientious hunters, but that there were also many indolent and lazy individuals who lived off the results of other people's efforts. He described them collectively as "a happy go-lucky race" and said that "it takes many hungry days, and dark ones, to drive out all their fun."

The first summer the *Albert* was in the harbour that bore its name, whaling and trading were poor. Mutch wrote about it: "We did not have much chance to make a good fishing as the pack came in on the boats. And the only time the whales came the ships [i.e., larger ships] were there to help catch them. The *Eclipse* got one at the time referred to. And the *Diana* one. And we got one but small, then long after the *Eclipse* another but very small. We got one on the 19th of June." In writing about the narwhal-tusk trade, he noted that "the best I have seen is 8 feet long and about 18 lbs. They have heavy bodies at that weight of horn and lots of blubber." He also took a few white whales and walruses.

The year 1905 was an even poorer one for whaling and hunting from the station. "My year's catch has been the worst I have had yet," he wrote. "No whale bone at all, as I had only, or was only able to save about 50 narwhals out of 150 we shot, i.e. the ice took the others away from us. And the winter was so bad they got but a few seals, and we only managed to salt 218. We had 22 bearskins, 13 walrus hides and almost 280 lbs of narwhal horns—that's the voyage of 1905."

In the fall, Mutch took passage back to Scotland aboard another Dundee whaler, the *Eclipse*, leaving the *Albert* and its crew to winter and continue whaling and trading the following year. "The *Albert* was left in a harbour," Mutch wrote, "men to look after the stations, and to whale till the ice made, and get the boats ready for the spring whaling which begins about the last of May, and to put the boats down whither [sic] I be back in time or not. If the whaling is good for the *Albert* she will be home this year to get an engine of some kind into her. That was the arrangement about a month ago."

Mutch returned the following year, again travelling on the *Eclipse*, commanded by Captain W. F. Milne. But plans had changed, and the *Albert* did not go to Scotland to be refitted with an engine. Instead, Mutch and the crew remained in the far North for one more winter. In 1907, he finally moved the little ship out of its comfortable harbour, its home for three winters, and took it back to Scotland.

The following year, Mutch purchased the vessel from Mitchell's Dundee Pond's Bay Company and, with some Peterhead associates, formed his own enterprise, the Albert Whaling Company.

Thus ended the four-year adventure of Mutch, his ship, and the Cumberland Sound Inuit who had pioneered whaling from a fixed shore base in the High Arctic. As a whaling venture, it hadn't been terribly successful. Commercial bowhead whaling in the Arctic was nearing an end, morphing into a hunt for beluga, narwhal, and walrus, and into trading for skins and tusks, and even that was a dicey proposition.

There were unexpected effects of this adventure on the Inuit of Pond's Bay. The Cumberland Sound Inuit, the Uqqurmiut, had had contact with Christianity—the Blacklead Island mission station, where many of them had lived in Cumberland Sound, had been established some years before the northern voyage of the *Albert*. Some of the Uqqurmiut, though not all, had already converted to the new religion. Many were literate in syllabics. And so the message of Christianity and the gift of literacy would have been passed on to the Tununirmiut during these years, long before the arrival of any white missionaries, an unexpected legacy of James Mutch's venture.

An Aging Whaler

Mutch purchased the *Albert* for £1,200, then exchanged her for six hundred shares in a new venture formed with associates in Peterhead, the Albert Whaling Company Limited. It was said that anyone in town who had any money contributed, in the vain hope of restoring Peterhead's reputation of the good old days when the town had flourished as a great whaling port.

Mutch decided that, with this new venture, he would return to Peterhead every fall—there would be no more wintering in the Arctic. This was a sensible move, for he was by then sixty-one years of age.

In 1908, he went out on a summer hunting voyage to Davis Strait. The following year, he was again in the strait, hunting off Disco Island, which the whalers knew as the Whale Fish Islands.

In 1910, he hunted off Sukkertoppen, Greenland, and off Kivitoo on the Baffin coast. There he met the famous Norwegian explorer Otto Sverdrup, who visited his ship. Beset by unfavourable winds in the ice off Kivitoo—the *Albert* still had no engine—the vessel had to be towed out by another Scottish ship, the *Diana*, on October 5. The summer had not been a success. Mutch returned to Peterhead with 202 walrus hides but no whalebone.

Mutch left the Albert Whaling Company and the little ship that he loved in 1911 and went to a competitor, the Sabellum Company, based in London. From that year on, his efforts would be devoted more to trading than to whaling, and to dealing with Inuit middlemen whom he would supply on annual voyages. In that first year with Sabellum, he established a trading post at Cape Mercy. Others would follow. An Inuk known as Durban Harry looked after his interests at Durban Harbour near Padloping. The famed Kanaaka was his middleman in Cumberland Sound. Niaquttiaq and his wife, Qaunnaq (who served also as Mutch's girlfriend), looked after the post that he built at Kivitoo.

Two years later, on the vessel *Erme*, the aging Mutch returned to Kekerten in Cumberland Sound for the first time in thirteen years. He rescued the crew of the *Ernest William*, which had been wrecked there, and took them and a stranded missionary, E. W. T. Greenshield, back to England.

In 1918, Mutch left Ireland, again aboard the *Erme*, bound for Baffin Island. But the vessel was torpedoed by a German U-boat and sank. Mutch survived.

In 1922, Mutch falsified his sea records, claiming to be sixty-seven instead of his actual age of seventy-five, and set out once again for Davis Strait in the little ship *Vera*. He visited his station at Cape Haven, but ice prevented him from getting to Kivitoo. The vessel was damaged, and he made for Sisimiut (then known as Holsteinsborg) on the Greenland coast. During repairs there, the *Vera* keeled over and broke her mast on a sheer cliff at the edge of the harbour. She filled with water and was declared unsalvageable. Mutch and his crew spent a number of weeks there awaiting passage back to Europe aboard a Danish supply ship.

While there, Mutch took many of his meals with the local administrator, and he and the *Vera*'s crew stayed at a building built in about 1906 for use as a hospital. To while away the time, some of his men made a crude sign for the building and nailed it up between two windows, just under the eaves. It read "VERA VILLA," and underneath that was written the standard abbreviation for Peterhead and the year: "PHD 1922."

My good friend, the late Ulrik Lennert, whose father salvaged wood from the wreck of the *Vera* and built a beautiful table from it (a table that Ulrik treasured in the years that I knew him), took me some years ago to show me this sign. The building—now a kindergarten, building B-17—is painted red, and so is the sign. That makes it difficult to photograph. But it is still there, though one has to look hard to find it.

That was James Mutch's last voyage to the Arctic. He began a well-deserved retirement in Peterhead. Two years later, his daughter's husband, Francis McRobbie, was killed in a boiler explosion, and the next year his widow, Jeannie, moved to South Africa. In 1927, Mutch, then aged eighty, and his wife followed their daughter. He spent his final years living at Rindebeach, a suburb of Cape Town. He died there in 1931, far from the Arctic to which he had devoted most of his adult years.

Those Inuit who knew him personally have all passed away, but many of their children, from Iqaluit to Pond Inlet, remember stories they heard from their elders about this remarkable man, Jiimi Maatsi.

James Mutch on the Map

The honour that all explorers yearn for is to have a spot on the map—or a number of spots—named for them. Some achieve it surreptitiously, as the whaler William Penny did when he named the Penny Highlands, modestly and unconvincingly claiming that he named the area after his father! Some achieve it while still living, as was the case when the scientist J. Dewey Soper named Mount Duval and the Duval River after the aging but still-living whaler William Duval. Some achieve it after death, whether that death came about peacefully at home in bed after a life of sterling accomplishment, or prematurely by accident. The latter is the case with the plethora of places named after the unfortunate Sir John Franklin, who perished in the Arctic.

Perhaps the greatest and rarest honour was to have Inuit themselves recommend an official place name. It was all the more exceptional when Inuit named a place after a Qallunaaq. But that is exactly what happened in the case of James Mutch, known to the Inuit as Jiimi Maatsi.

In 1975, Dr. G. V. B. Cochran, a member of the Explorers Club in New York who had climbed mountains on Bylot Island, wrote to the Secretariat for Geographical Names of the federal department Energy Mines and Resources Canada, suggesting the name Dundee Glacier for a certain glacier in northern Baffin Island. (For the record, the glacier is at 72°27'40" north latitude and 76°04'10" west longitude.) Cochran also suggested that two lakes in the area be named Firth Lakes or Portage Lakes. The department took four years to reject Cochran's suggestions, but ultimately they were all formally turned down on April 9, 1979. That's because the department had, in the meantime, asked the opinion of the Hamlet Council of Pond Inlet.

Simon Merkosak was the Secretary-Manager of the hamlet at the time, and he wrote on behalf of the council to the department that same year relating, in much abbreviated form, the story of James Mutch. In part he wrote, "Some years ago there was a whaler called by Inuit Jimi Maasi [Jiimi Maatsi] and he had two Inuit assistants, Alianakuluk and Inuutiq. They were ship wrecked in Erik Harbour and stayed there for a period of time."

The reference to a shipwreck is not quite accurate, but this brief statement contains some very important information. Mutch left no record of the names of the Inuit of northern Baffin Island who helped him, and this is the only record we have of the names of two of his Inuit assistants.

The council suggested that the two lakes be named Lake Inuutiq and Lake Alianakuluk, and that the glacier be named Jimi Maasi Glacier. These names were approved by the department on

August 2, 1979, fitting memorials for a legendary Scottish whaler and two of the Inuit who worked with him.

Let's hope, as the Inuit Heritage Trust carries out its mandate to ensure that Inuit place names are recognized, that Jimi Maasi Glacier remains on the map and that future generations remember that this name was put forward by Inuit themselves.

George Comer
The White Shaman

G eorge Comer was Canadian born but moved as a young man from Quebec to Connecticut with his mother. Born in 1858, he was only seventeen when he made his first whaling voyage, on the *Nile*, bound for Cumberland Sound. A fourteen-year hiatus from the Arctic followed, but he was at sea for most of that time, venturing as far away as the Antarctic on sealing trips.

The Antarctic experience readied Comer for the career that was to follow in the eastern Canadian Arctic. When he returned to the North, it was for three seasons as mate aboard the schooner *Era*, sailing out of New London, Connecticut, under his old master, Captain John Spicer. These were not whaling voyages, but rather trips to provision the whaling stations operated by the C. A. Williams firm. Williams's stations were usually manned by two white men; they employed Inuit crews in whaling, and also traded for their hunting and trapping products. The *Era* brought provisions, coal, and trade goods, and took home the products of the previous season.

In 1893, Comer had his first taste of an Arctic winter. He sailed aboard the *Canton* to Hudson Bay, a voyage that lasted fifteen months. The ship wintered at Depot Island, just to the north of Chesterfield Inlet, and Comer had his first opportunity to interact with Inuit for a protracted period of time.

In 1895, he was finally master in his own right, taking over as captain of the ship with which he was so familiar, the *Era*. He took her to Hudson Bay and wintered near Cape Fullerton. He would come to know the area and its Inuit well, for on each of his following three voyages, all as master of the same ship, he wintered there for two consecutive years.

American whaling in Hudson Bay had begun in 1860 as a result of the American experience in Cumberland Sound in the previous decade. That first year, two American ships wintered at Depot Island. When they returned south, one of them carried a larger amount of whalebone than any American ship had ever taken in the Davis Strait and Cumberland Sound fishery, and the other was not far behind. This news spread like wildfire in New England. In the following decade, there were fifty-seven American whaling voyages to Hudson Bay.

But whales were a finite resource, and stocks declined quickly. The Scots were late coming to Hudson Bay, but when they did, they exploited the same stocks that the Americans continued to deplete. By the time Comer arrived, whale stocks were seriously diminished. He took whales, to be sure, but he also traded extensively with the Inuit for the products of their hunt on land and sea.

Still, Comer was that rarity in these difficult times—a whaler whose voyages almost all turned a profit for his employer. On his

1897 voyage, for example, which wintered twice at Fullerton, he took 15 whales, which yielded 185 barrels of oil and 18,000 pounds of whalebone. On his voyage in 1900, he brought home 130 barrels of oil and 7,000 pounds of bone, but also 398 muskox skins, 69 wolf pelts, 51 polar bear skins, and 8 wolverine skins. Every bit of land produce helped offset the decline in whale products.

Comer employed Inuit to complement the work of his American crew. Most were Aivilingmiut, as they were native to the Fullerton area. But he also hired Netsilingmiut and Qairnirmiut, who had come to Fullerton Harbour for the employment and trade opportunities. During the long winters, he got to know them. He got on well with them and developed considerable fluency in their language. In 1912, he wrote in his journal while wintering on the *A. T. Gifford*: "Some of the native men come in to the cabin most every evening and I tell them about the outside world, or what the white people do, and also give them Bible stories or ancient history. In this way I get many stories from them of their customs and traditions."

George Comer was far more than just a whaleman. He was also an astute observer of the Inuit and their customs, with a passion for photography, which he started as early as 1893. An Inuk, Joe Curley, told the researcher Dorothy Eber, "I remember Captain Comer. We used to call him Angakkuq—the shaman—because he was able to take photographs. They would appear just like that, out of a piece of paper." And Leah Arnaujaq of Repulse Bay remembered, "Ah, Angakkuq, with his little bald head; he was a shamanistic person!" Kanajuq Bruce in Coral Harbour told Eber in the 1980s, "Angakkuq was a very likeable man. He got his name because of the photographs and because he had those little technical things that would wind up. People here never used to have those mechanical things."

"Those mechanical things" included gramophones, with which he entertained the Inuit, and devices on which he recorded traditional songs, dances, and stories on sixty-four wax cylinders. These were the first sound recordings of North American Inuit.

Through Captain John Spicer, Comer had been introduced to the anthropologist Franz Boas, and he began collecting artifacts, clothing, skeletal material, and legends for the American Museum of Natural History, where Boas was employed. Comer made 220 plaster casts of Inuit for the museum; 177 of them were faces. His photographic collections survive today as glass plate negatives at Mystic Seaport, Connecticut, and as prints at the natural history museum. He never felt comfortable collecting skulls and skeletons, despite Boas's constant requests.

Like James Mutch, the Scotsman who also collected for Boas, Comer was a rough and untutored ethnographer. Our knowledge of the material and intellectual culture of the Inuit of western Hudson Bay owes much to him.

Comer eventually retired to his home in East Haddam, Connecticut, a home filled with memorabilia from the North. He died there in 1937.

* * *

Much has been written about Comer and his relationship with an Inuit woman, Siusaarnaq, more commonly known as Nivissannaq. Of course, both of these names were too difficult for the whalers to pronounce, and so they called her Shoofly. She was one of the wives—he had two—of an Inuit man named Auqqajaq—the whalers called him Ben—who worked with Comer as his assistant. In fact, Ben had saved Comer's life early in his Hudson Bay career. Comer had fallen through thin ice up to his waist, a result of inexperience in the ways of the country. Trying to get out, he compounded his problem by losing his rifle in the water. "This is the man who pulled me out of the water when I had broken through the thin ice and to whose timely arrival I owe my life," Comer wrote. It was February 1894, and the air temperature hovered around -30°F. The ship was four miles away. Ben loaded Comer onto a sled and raced the dogs back to the ship.

Shoofly owed her nickname to a popular song, "Shoo Fly, Don't Bother Me." A grandson living on Southampton Island claimed, "Her captain gave her that name because she was always shooing away the flies." She and Ben had one son, John Ell. His name, too, was one given him by whalers; he was named after John L. Sullivan, a popular American boxer.

Shoofly's younger sister, Ukkuq, had had a long-standing relationship with Comer. The result of the liaison was a son, Pamiulik, who later took the first name Laurent. Ukkuq died while giving birth to Comer's second child, who also died during the birth. Pamiulik was Comer's only child in the Arctic.

It was not uncommon for a senior assistant to a whaling captain to share his wife with the captain, and so, after Ukkuq's death, Shoofly lived aboard ship with Comer whenever he was in the country. Her granddaughter, Bernadette Ookpik Patterk, the daughter of Shoofly's only child, John Ell, dispelled any suggestion that John Ell was actually Comer's son, as some have written: "Yes, my grandmother had a captain friend," she told Dorothy Eber. "But it was after John Ell was born that Angakkuq [Comer] was living with Shoofly. My grandmother could bear no more children. John Ell had no Qallunaaq blood. He was true Inuit." She explained further, "Ben knew the captain had Nivissannaq as a girlfriend, but they were real good friends to each other." Joe Curley, the son of another Inuk who worked for whalers, said, "I can't tell you for how many years Shoofly and Angakkuq were living together, but they were always together. Whenever he came up here she would travel with the captain. They were looked upon as man and wife."

Shoofly is also well-remembered as an excellent seamstress who taught younger Inuit traditional skills. Joe Curley said, "She was a wise person. . . . People looked to her for advice, and she was really good at dealing with people. . . . She was regarded as one of the leaders among our people."

Ben died in June 1905, and Comer assisted at his burial, writing, "Our native Ben who has been sick died this afternoon. My boat's crew and I went up to the tent as he was a man whom all liked. I helped carry him away and assisted in the burial."

After Ben's death, and probably after Comer had departed the region, Shoofly took another husband, Angutimmarik, known to the whalers as Scotch Tom because he had always worked for the Scottish whalers rather than the Americans.

Comer left the North for good in 1919. But John Ell wrote to him, apparently often. In 1933, he had Sam Ford of the Hudson's Bay Company send the captain a letter in which he thanked him for a box of items sent the previous summer and gave him some news, including the sad news that his mother was in failing health. John Ell reported that he was employed by the Hudson's Bay Company and had purchased a large boat. He asked Comer to send him three barrels of gasoline and some Winchester rifles. "If you send me this I will be very glad," he closed.

Shoofly died in the 1930s. She and George Comer—Angakkuq, the shaman—are still remembered with respect by the Inuit of the Kivalliq region.

Saved by Inuit, Rescued by Whalers

Shipwreck at Blacklead Island

The flag of Nunavut flew over a school in Germany for a week in 2011 to mark the one hundredth anniversary of the death of a man in Baffin Island. The distinctive red-and-white emblem flew over the Grundschule Bernhard Hantzsch, an elementary school in Kurort Hartha in Saxony, a school named after a German ornithologist, the first white man to cross Baffin Island, who died on the shores of Foxe Basin sometime in late May or early June 1911.

In July 1909, the small two-masted schooner *Jantina Agatha*, out of Groningen, Holland, left Dundee under the command of Captain Cornelis Dijkstra, carrying provisions for the whaling and mission station at Blacklead Island in Arctic Canada. The cargo consisted of twenty tons of coal and an equal amount of general supplies. Dijkstra, described as "a quiet, almost cool-blooded person," had a good reputation in the Groningen coastal shipping world, and carried a diploma for high-seas sailing vessels.

Accompanying the crew of five were two passengers, the Reverend E. W. T. Greenshield, who had been on furlough, and the German ornithologist Bernhard Hantzsch.

Hantzsch had been born in Dresden in 1875, the youngest son of a schoolteacher. He developed an interest in bird life at an early age. In 1897, he took a position as a teacher and published his first paper on ornithology the same year. In later years, he travelled to the Balkans and Bulgaria to further his research, and in 1903 made a study trip to Iceland, where he identified two subspecies of birds unknown to ornithology. In 1906, he was in Labrador and Killinek (Port Burwell) and subsequently published two papers on the results of his research there.

The trip aboard the *Jantina Agatha* was uneventful until the ship hit ice and began taking on water on the night of September 25, still fifty miles from Blacklead. The crew made a valiant attempt to pump, but soon decided that they would have to abandon ship. The captain gave the order to get Hantzsch's heavy German naval sloop out of the hold. With six feet of water in the ship, Dijkstra remained calm. The sloop afloat, he ordered his men to load it with the supplies that he and Greenshield selected from the large stock of provisions.

The *Jantina Agatha*, listing slightly to starboard, still held tons of cargo that would be desperately needed if an over-wintering became necessary, but the sloop was soon full. A futile effort was made to build a raft on which to carry more supplies. Maps, compasses, and rifles were taken from the doomed vessel into the ship's boats, and, at six o'clock on the evening of September 27, Dijkstra remarked almost offhandedly, "I'd say we'd better get off."

The crew took to the perilous waters of Cumberland Sound in three small boats. They rowed for almost twelve hours before reaching a small island. After a night's sleep there, Dijkstra, Greenshield, and two others rowed on to Blacklead to fetch help.

Blacklead Island was the site of a large Inuit settlement. In its heyday it had been a thriving whaling station and the site of a mission station of the Church Missionary Society. Whaling was in decline, and no white missionary had been at the station since Greenshield had left the previous year. But over one hundred Inuit remained there, anticipating the return of the whalers and the missionary that fall.

The four shipwrecked men reached Blacklead safely, and a party of Inuit in two whaleboats left almost immediately to take provisions to the hapless sailors left on the small island. They rowed for eighteen hours to rescue them. They, with the rescued men, returned to Blacklead in the early hours of October 1.

The Dutch sailors, German scientist, and British preacher were forced to spend an unexpected winter on the island, poorly supplied, for no other ships put in at Blacklead that fall.

An Uncomfortable Winter at Blacklead Island

The entire party lived in the tiny mission quarters with Reverend Greenshield, the only one who could speak Inuktitut. He was concerned greatly about food, feeling that what they had salvaged would be enough to feed only one man for a year. By mid-winter, the food situation was desperate. The Inuit on the island hunted for their own families and generously provided the white men with whatever food they could, primarily seal meat, but sometimes there was not enough for all. But no matter how little the hunters caught, they always remembered the white men and provided them with something.

The sailors slept long into the mornings during that desperate winter, both to forget their hunger and to save coal. By late spring, they were getting two ship's biscuits and a few bowls of seal broth a day. Later this was reduced to one biscuit and an occasional piece of seal meat. They had long since exchanged their European clothing for Inuit sealskin garments. Other than hunger, the greatest hardship was excruciating boredom. They socialized with the Inuit and one evening taught them to play musical chairs. In the dead of winter, they constructed a billiard table, made of a door with a blanket stretched over it. Cushions were made from wire and the down of eider ducks. An Inuk made the balls from whale rib and the cues from wood tipped with walrus ivory and India rubber. Billiards was a popular pastime for a while after that.

But the months seemed like years. At many points in this winter of hardship, the shipwrecked sailors feared for their very survival. They thought of home, in the sure knowledge that everyone there would have thought them dead. This knowledge weighed heavily on them. One wrote in his diary, "It is to die here. For there is nothing here." Even as spring approached, they all knew that if a ship did not reach them that summer, they would probably not survive another winter.

Amazingly, throughout all this, the German ornithologist, Bernhard Hantzsch, jealously guarded his own supplies, which he had managed to save from the *Jantina Agatha* before it sank. It was his plan to go inland in the spring, through to Foxe Basin on a three-year expedition, and he refused to share his supplies with any of the desperate sailors. But not only did he refuse to share, he also insisted on eating with the sailors out of the common rations, while saving all his supplies for his own trip. The sailors felt that they had a right to Hantzsch's supplies, as they had salvaged them from the sinking ship. They threatened the scientist with harm, and he begged Greenshield not to leave him alone with them. Finally, he agreed to give up some biscuits and a little tobacco. One of the Dutch sailors referred to him with understatement in his diary as "not a greatly beloved man in the small colony."

Later, while travelling with Inuit in the interior of Baffin Island, en route to Foxe Basin, Hantzsch would have an unpleasant surprise. Along with his other supplies, he was carrying a number of cases of canned food. Upon opening a case, he discovered that the desperate Dutch sailors had surreptitiously opened some of his cans, removed the food, and replaced it with stones to provide the expected weight, before returning the cans to their cases.

Rescue, and a Queen's Generosity

The shipwrecked Dutch sailors were happy to see Hantzsch leave Blacklead for Foxe Basin with his guides in April 1910. The missionary was relieved, too, for he had often been called upon to intervene in disputes between the sailors and the scientist, usually over food. Hantzsch died the following spring on the lonely shores of Foxe Basin.

By early June, the sailors knew that their survival, if not their rescue, was assured. The weather had warmed, and the Inuit took some of the sailors on a hunting and fishing expedition. Two boats, each crewed by eight men, left the island, taking with them two sleds and sixteen dogs. This venture lasted two weeks and was a success. They shot seals and polar bears before crossing Cumberland Sound and taking twelve caribou. On the return trip, they were able to shoot a walrus and even a whale. A week later, a number of the stranded sailors went out again with the Inuit, this time for eggs.

In August, two whalers from Dundee, first the *Thomas*, then the *Scotia*, reached Blacklead. The *Thomas* was too small to carry all the sailors, so only the cook and an ordinary seaman went on her. The rest of the party waited at the mission while the *Scotia* whaled in the sound, taking them aboard later in the season for the return trip to Scotland.

The mate of the *Jantina Agatha* sent a letter home on the *Thomas*. "You are now celebrating over there," he wrote, in reference to the festivities accompanying a Dutch holiday, "but we are doing so no less, for there are as many as two steamers and a sailing ship here. We now live in abundance. Truly the need was great; the people here were eating dogs to satisfy their hunger."

The sailors arrived in Dundee, to great curiosity, wearing Inuit sealskin garments. By early October, all of them had returned safely to Groningen.

Earlier that summer, they had been given up for dead. Their wives had already been promised compensation by the Seamen's College. The daughter of the second mate recalled years later, "We heard little from Father about it. He'd rather not mention that trip. Life among the Eskimos must have been hard. He did say emotionally once: 'They are the very best people in the world.' They were treated extremely well there. The people there were completely unselfish."

Greenshield returned to England on the *Scotia* in the fall of 1910. The following summer, he went out again to Blacklead. He took with him some unexpected supplies. Earlier that year, Queen Wilhelmina of the Netherlands, having heard the story of the selfless care Greenshield and the Inuit had given her stranded countrymen, had made the missionary a Knight of the Order of Orange Nassau.

The letter he received from the Dutch Consul-General in London, informing him of the queen's decree, added that the queen was also granting him an allowance of two hundred guilders, "which is intended to enable you to supply some of the goods which would be appreciated by your Eskimos as a mark of appreciation of the kindness displayed by them towards our shipwrecked mariners."

As soon as the *Scotia* had left Blacklead, Greenshield distributed the supplies he had purchased, explaining to the Inuit that "the gifts were sent in appreciation of the splendid spirit of self-denial shown by them" and "that they came from the Queen herself." Greenshield's biography records that "the natives received their presents with many words of thanks."

The Murrays
of Peterhead
A Whaling Family

The Murrays of Peterhead, Scotland, were a whaling family. Alexander Murray had a large family; two of his sons followed him into the whaling trade, and both of them became captains in their own right. Alexander Junior, the elder son, was born May 21, 1860, and John was born eight years later, on July 26, 1868.

In 1884, Alexander Senior was captain of the *Windward*, and on that voyage he took his fifteen-year-old son John along. It was the boy's first experience of whaling. The following year he sailed, again with his father, on the *Perseverance* to Cumberland Sound, where the ship wintered. This voyage was not commercially successful, for the ship took only one whale, which yielded one ton of whalebone and twenty tons of oil. They also took four hundred seals and twelve walruses.

In Those Days

In 1887, John sailed on a merchant ship around the Horn and up to San Francisco. He was gone for two and a half years and also visited Australia, Chile, and England. But he returned to whaling after this adventure.

The Hudson's Bay Company (HBC) had purchased his old ship, the *Perseverance*, and in 1891, John Murray signed on as an able-bodied seaman for a supply voyage to Hudson Bay. That winter he got his second mate's certificate in Aberdeen, and the following year joined the same ship, for which his older brother Alexander Junior was now the captain. They wintered at Repulse Bay and returned to Peterhead the following summer with the produce of 4 whales and 235 sealskins.

By 1894, John had his first mate's ticket and signed on to the *Perseverance* in that capacity, again under his brother. This was another wintering voyage, this time at Depot Island, and it was unusual in that Alexander took his young wife, Helen, along. A white woman in the Arctic was a rarity, and the Inuit flocked to the ship to inspect her. John Murray's son, Austin, recalled: "The Eskimo women were delighted to hear that a white woman had come. They crowded the decks to see her. She waited and kept them waiting, and then came out on the arm of her husband dressed in her best dress with fashionable balloon sleeves. The Eskimo women were captivated; so happy. Then she gave each one of them several yards of good cotton and they all made ballooned sleeved dresses for themselves and came back a few days later to show them to Mrs. Murray. They were terrific craftswomen."

Helen Murray gave birth to her first child, Alexander Percy, on the *Perseverance* in 1895. John returned to London that summer with his sister-in-law and her baby, leaving his brother in Hudson Bay. By 1896, John had his own master's ticket, and he came out on the HBC supply vessel *Erik* to relieve his brother on the *Perseverance*. He wintered again at Repulse Bay and returned home the following summer. The whaling adventure of the HBC had not been a commercial success, and the company later sold the ship.

In 1897, John and Alexander sailed together again, John as mate, his older brother as captain, on the Dundee vessel *Active*. A telling statement in a biography of John Murray indicates the decline of the whaling business: "By 1898 whales had become so scarce that ships were killing anything that would produce a profit and this voyage the *Active* was looking for walruses." She took 150 walruses, in addition to 17 polar bears, but no whales. It is doubtful if there was any profit to the voyage.

In 1899, John Murray took a group of Aivilingmiut to Southampton Island and remained there for three winters. This was perhaps his most controversial venture. A few years later, a Dundee paper paraphrased A. P. Low of the Canadian government steamer *Neptune*, who had been in Hudson Bay in 1903, as follows:

Professor A. P. Low . . . describes the extinction of a tribe of Eskimos on Southampton Island . . . in a single winter. They numbered one hundred souls, and made shift to live with fair success without employing civilised implements of war or chase, as they were isolated from any neighbours. But in 1900 a Scottish whaling firm established a station there, and managed it with a party of Eskimos from one of its other posts who could use a modern repeating rifle successfully. These recklessly slaughtered the musk oxen and the deer of the region for the sake of the hide, which they sold to their whaling employers, and as a result the whole of the original tribe perished of starvation during the second winter, while the others, who were morally responsible for their death, if not legally punishable, survived through the aid of the provisions furnished to them by their employers. Two years later the whaling station was abandoned again, and now this large island is absolutely unpeopled.[1]

Of course, the story of the extinction of the Sadlermiut is more complicated than that. Still, it is telling that a newspaper in a Scottish whaling port published such an indictment of John Murray and his immigrant Aivilingmiut.

John Murray himself was an accomplished hunter and marksman. Late in life, he claimed that he had killed 103 polar bears over his Arctic career.

One can pretty well reconstruct Alexander Junior's return trips to Scotland and his subsequent winterings there by looking at the birthdates of the children that resulted. His son Alexander Percy was born in Hudson Bay in 1895, but five more children were born back home in Scotland, in 1898, 1900, 1902, 1906, and 1910. But Alexander was also busy on the domestic front while in Hudson Bay. He employed many Inuit in whale and walrus hunting, and they came aboard each summer, many with their families. Alexander took up with a woman named Ooloota from the Cape Dorset area, and she gave birth to two of his children, Isaacie Ikidluak and Leah Arnauyak.

Leah Arnauyak spent her final years in Repulse Bay and knew exactly who her white father was. She told the historian Dorothy Eber that she knew John Murray—the Inuit called him Nakungajuq, "the Cross-eyed One"—better, "but Alexander was

---

[1] Anonymous, "A Vanishing Race," *Dundee Courier* (November 20, 1907), 5.

my father." Ikidluak told Eber, "I was born when the ship *Active* was coming up around here. My father was the captain of the ship, Captain Murray. I have heard that was his name though I don't remember him. I used to think that my mother's husband was my real father. His whaling name was Iyola and his baptized name was Abraham. Yes, I remember going on the *Active*—just little bits."

The *Active* played a big role in the lives of many Inuit families on the north shore of Hudson Strait and in Repulse Bay. An elderly lady, Anirnik, in Cape Dorset, told Eber:

> I was born on the *Active*. When I was a little girl we were on the *Active* every year and all summer because my father was hunting bowhead whales in Arvilik—the land of big whales. When we saw the smoke we started to pack our things to be ready to board the ship. . . . There were many men helping my father and there used to be lots of us sleeping in the hold. . . . There were no white people in the hold—only the Inuit. The Qallunaat had their living quarters in the front and the back of the ship.[2]

The *Active* even had its own Inuit name, *Umiarjuarapik*—"the beautiful ship."

Alexander Murray's double life came to a sudden end on November 11, 1912. He was still in command of the *Active* and was planning to winter in the Ottawa Islands in Hudson Bay. His nephew, Austin Murray, recounted that Alexander "lost his life on the

---

[2] Dorothy Harley Eber, *When the Whalers Were Up North* (Montreal & Kingston: McGill-Queen's University Press, 1989), 90.

ice, hunting caribou. He'd been out a long time and got very hot, sweaty, very thirsty and when he got the chance of some water, it was ice-water—and he drank too fast. He died on the spot. It was so cold it went through his system like a knife."

After his older brother's death, John Murray continued to be active in the Arctic. For many years, he was in command of the tiny *Albert* for Henry Toke Munn's Arctic Gold Exploration Syndicate, but by this time whaling had ceased to be whaling and evolved into what is generally called free trading. He worked for Revillon Freres, a trading company that was a serious rival to the HBC, for four years. Later, he worked for the HBC itself for a short time. He retired to Wormit, across the Tay River from Dundee, in 1934, and died there in 1948.

The Dead
Horse Song

Arctic whalers were a superstitious lot and had their own rituals that they carried out aboard ship, especially en route to the whaling grounds.

One ceremony was "The Dead Horse Song," celebrated on whaling ships in the 1800s.

Late in life, Austin Murray, son of the well-known Arctic whaling captain John Murray, recounted the ceremony as he had heard it from his father:

Ordinary sailors got a month's "advance" when they signed on a ship. This was often spent before they set sail or given to the wife or family. Thus, starting out on a new voyage sailors used to feel that, for the first month, they were working for nothing—"working out the dead horse." So on certain ships it was traditional that on the last evening of this first month . . . a procession would appear on deck carrying torches and holding the stuffed effigy of a horse made of canvas. Astride this "hobby-horse" one of the sailors would dance about waving a whip, or he might be dragged round by the other sailors. This man would be wearing old clothes and a battered tall hat. And there was this song:

> They say old man, your horse will die,
> And they say so, and they hope so.
> They say old man, your horse will die!
> O, poor old horse.
> Then if he dies I'll tan your hide,
> And they say so, and they hope so.
> And if he lives, I'll ride him again,
> O, poor old horse.
>
> Old horse, old horse, what brought you here
> After carrying sand for many a year
> From Bantry Bay to Ballywhack,
> Where you fell down and broke your back?
> Now, after years of such abuse,
> They salt you down for sailors' use;
> They tan your hide and burn your bones,
> And send you off to Davy Jones.

And afterwards the "hobby-horse" would be run up to the lee main yardarm, where a man would be ready with a blue light and a knife. He'd fire the light and cut the rope holding the stuffed hobby-horse, which would plunge down into the sea to big cheers from the whole crew. That was a very old custom.[1]

Austin Murray never visited the Arctic, where his father spent so many years. But he vividly recalled the tales his father had told him of the last days of whaling among the Inuit in Hudson Bay and Davis Strait. It was my privilege to visit Austin Murray in Scotland in late 2003, a few months before his death.

---

[1]Austin Murray, "The Last of the Dundee Whalers," in Timothy Neat, *When I Was Young: Voices from Lost Communities in Scotland—the Highlands and East Coast* (Edinburgh: Birlinn, 2001), 231–73.

David Cardno

At Home in Cumberland Sound

Stowaway

Running away from home is probably the dream of every young boy at some point in his life. But in 1866, thirteen-year-old David Cardno turned his dream into reality when he successfully stowed away—after two unsuccessful attempts in the previous two years—on a whaling ship bound from Peterhead, Scotland, to Cumberland Sound in the far-off Canadian Arctic.

On his second attempt, David had gotten as far as Lerwick in Shetland before being sent back with a dozen other young Peterhead boys, each given a lump of salt beef and some ship's biscuits to tide them over on their way home.

David's reason for going to the Arctic was simple. His father was in Cumberland Sound, managing a shore station for a whaling company, and the teenager wanted to join him. So on June 14, 1866, he bade his mother goodbye and headed off to school—or so his mother thought. Instead, he concealed himself aboard a ship, the *Lord Saltoun*, owned by his father's employer. Undetected, he made his presence known only when well out to sea. Still, the captain would have sent him back from his first stop at Orkney, but the owner happened to be aboard and intervened, hiring the adventurous rascal as "ship's boy."

The *Lord Saltoun*, under Captain Alexander Murray Senior, reached Cumberland Sound after a stormy Atlantic passage. Her first stop was a small whaling station called Lucas Harbour, where Murray expected to unite young Cardno with his father. But Cardno Senior was away, and Murray surmised that he was across the sound at Kekerten. Murray left David and a crew member, Keith Milne, at Lucas Harbour and departed for that station.

The next morning, the teenager had his first meeting with Inuit. In his memoirs, he recounted the events this way:

I was aroused very early, before daylight, by the noise of voices outside, all chattering together in a strange tongue. I jumped out of bed and was over at the window in an instant. Peering out into the gloom, I received the shock of my life, for within a few yards of the station what appeared to be a whole colony of people had settled down overnight. I could discern a cluster of huts, and all around squat, furred people, most of them moving about in a haphazard fashion, and all of them talking at once.

"Do you think they'll kill us, Keith?" I whispered.

"Na, na; they surely winna dae that," he replied, much to my relief, for although I knew that the people were the

Eskimos of whom I had heard so much, I was not very clear about their attitude to white people.[1]

David and Keith prepared a soup of peas and barley and served all their visitors, who numbered over a hundred men, women, and children. They stayed a number of days, and David Cardno made the first of many lasting friendships with them. He also spent every spare moment learning to handle a kayak, a skill at which he would become proficient.

Another week passed before the *Lord Saltoun* returned with David's father. David described the encounter as "a strange meeting in a strange part of the world." He wrote that "although my father was not entirely pleased at my exploit, I knew he was glad to see me. . . . He did not reprove me much, and I felt I had been forgiven for running away."

The *Lord Saltoun* took no whales that season. Worse, the ice in the sound closed in early that fall, and the ship had to winter at Naujartalik (Niantilik Harbour to the whalers), along with six other Scottish and American vessels. David Cardno's adventure turned into a year-long sojourn among the Inuit, the first of many in his long and adventurous life.

A Boy's Life in Cumberland Sound

Young David made friends with all of the Inuit of Naujartalik, but one family with two young boys became his particular friends. Years later he recalled the joys of his carefree time with this family:

---

[1] David Cardno, "My Forty Years in the Cruel Arctic," *People's Journal* (March 19, 1932).

We got a skin from their Mother and we had some great fun going up to the top of the hill, and laid the skin down on the snow and sat down on the skin, and we did come down that hill with some speed—our faces used to be covered with loose snow, the rate we came down. I may say I was nearly as much in their house as I was in the ship. When the father came home at night there was always a pan of boiled seal ready for him, so I came in for my share just the same as their own two, and I was picking up a word or two of their lingo, and when I felt very hungry I used to go to other igloos on Niantilik Island, as all the natives nearby lived there that was engaged to the ships. After we had dinner [on the ship], if there was any soup left, I got it from the cook into a beef tin and took it ashore and gave it to the children, and they did think a lot of that. [2]

One day, after being spanked by his father for arguing with some of the men over a card game, David embarked on his second runaway adventure. As he told it, "The teasing I got from the crew was unbearable and I had to get away. Looking over the side of the ship I saw a native I had met before, Murloo, a boat puller, who often came to Niantilik for provisions." Murloo was on his way back to the small island where he and his wife lived, twelve miles away. "As the sled passed within a few feet of the ship," Cardno wrote, "I dropped over the side and landed on top of it. Murloo was completely taken aback by my sudden appearance. 'I'm going with you,' I shouted."

---

[2] David Cardno, quoted in Marjory Harper, "Arctic Adventures," *Leopard Magazine* (December, 1989): 24–27.

In Those Days

Murloo agreed, and young Cardno lived for three weeks in a snow house with the man and his wife. "My new quarters were in a low hut made of frozen snow and lined with hides," Cardno recalled. "A seal oil lamp burned day and night keeping the place warm and comfortable. I made myself at home from the start and didn't give the consequences of my venture a second thought. That night, lying on a couch of deer skin, I slept as soundly as I ever did." He passed the time playing hunting games with spears and bows and arrows during the day, and playing cards and dominoes at night. The idyll ended when his father arrived to take him back to the ship.

But life on a whaling ship was not without its dangers, and David Cardno saw his share of disaster during his winter in Cumberland Sound. The *Dublin*, despite her name a Peterhead vessel, caught fire when a seal-oil lamp fell onto some books in a library belonging to the blacksmith. The ship had taken two whales, and the hold was filled with oil and blubber. When the flames reached the hold, an explosion occurred, and the ship burned to the water line.

On a trip across the sound to Kekerten, a sailor, Peter Corduff, froze his feet. Back at the ship, his badly frostbitten feet had to be amputated, a task performed by Johnny Bruce, the ship's cooper, with a sealing knife and without benefit of anaesthetic. Two other Scotsmen and a thirteen-year-old Inuit boy died on a similar attempt to cross the sound.

But David Cardno relished the winter's pleasures and survived its ordeals. On September 26, 1867, he and his father returned to Peterhead. Young Cardno wanted more, though. He wrote later, "My appetite for Arctic adventure was now stronger than ever and I couldn't wait for another chance to go North."

He would go to the Arctic many more times, often but not always to Cumberland Sound. His last voyage as an active member of a whaling crew was in 1898. Following that, he did local work herring fishing and trawling, and harbour construction at Peterhead.

But in 1910, at the age of fifty-seven, David Cardno would again sail for Cumberland Sound, this time to manage a shore station.

Trading at Kekerten and Blacklead

In 1910, David Cardno accepted an offer to manage the whaling station at Kekerten. Leaving his wife behind in Peterhead, and accompanied by George Miller, a local cooper, Cardno once again headed for the Arctic. Practically speaking, the bowhead whaling industry was at an end. The operation by that time was based mostly on sealing. Cardno described the fall hunt simply: "We launched our two boats before dawn each day and were back at the station by late afternoon with our catch. The small boats were crewed by natives and we hunted around the floe-edge, the outermost part of the ice."

The winter was a time of inactivity, but Cardno described the station as being cozy and with a good collection of books in the library. Often Inuit would come to the station and hold a dance in the kitchen to the music provided by Cardno's gramophone. Sealing would not begin again until May.

By the time the ship arrived in September, Cardno had a variety of skins salted in the storage sheds: 2,679 sealskins, 159 walrus hides, 15 beluga whale skins, 5 dogskins, 12 bearskins, 5 wolfskins, and 160 white fox pelts.

In Those Days

That fall, Cardno moved from Kekerten across Cumberland Sound to Blacklead Island, where he managed the station and had the company of the missionary E. W. T. Greenshield. He remained there for two years.

Cardno has left a good description of Hogmanay—as the Scots describe New Year's Eve—in 1912:

> Greenshield and I arranged a festive night for the 300 natives and we decorated the big hall for the occasion. We played cards, bagatelle [a type of billiards], dominoes, skittles, and quoits, and with the singing and dancing we all had a fine time. Gifts and toys had arrived for the German explorer [Bernhard Hantzsch] to trade with the natives, so we handed them out to our friends. The festivities went on until about four o'clock in the morning, when we finished off with a hymn and three cheers for our King and Queen. The following day I treated myself to a haunch of roast venison and a big plum duff! [3]

One day in August 1913, Cardno was at the lookout post on Signal Hill when he spotted the supply ship *Ernest William*. The ship was in such bad shape, however, that she had to be beached, and her crew was rescued by another vessel, the *Erme*, belonging to a competing company. That ship was not in much better shape, and nearly capsized on the homeward journey, with Cardno and the missionary, Greenshield, aboard. Captain Fletcher narrowly escaped death. The wave that almost capsized the ship swept him

---

[3] Gavin Sutherland (ed.), *A Whaler's Tale: The Memoirs of David Hawthorn Cardno of Peterhead* (Aberdeen: Aberdeenshire Council, 1996), 52.

overboard, but his legs became caught in a rope. When the ship righted itself, the first men on deck saw the captain being towed feet first behind the ship! They quickly hauled him aboard.

After twenty-six days at sea, the tiny vessel reached London on November 6, 1913, and David Cardno made his way home to Peterhead after an absence of three years.

Exile at Kekerten

David Cardno's return to Peterhead in the fall of 1913 didn't last long. Seven months later, on June 6, he left again for Cumberland Sound, this time in the employ of Robert Kinnes of Dundee, who had purchased Crawford Noble's whaling and trading stations. Cardno took charge of Kekerten, and another man from Peterhead, Jimmy Law, took over Blacklead Island. Although both men had been hired for two years, only one year's provisions had been sent, the idea being that a supply ship would come the following summer.

Three hundred Inuit lived at Kekerten. Cardno was known to most of them. He passed the winter pleasantly. He had a fresh supply of books, and thirteen Harry Lauder records for his gramophone. The Inuit mimicked the singing of the famous Scotsman, and were especially taken with his song "I Love a Lassie." It is likely that this Scots phrase is the origin of the Inuit woman's name Olassie.

Jimmy Law visited from Blacklead in April. His supplies had run out, so Cardno shared with him his remaining bread, tea, sugar, peas, barley, and biscuits. By mid-September, he regretted his generosity, because the supply ship had still not arrived and Cardno himself was now low on supplies. One day that month, he smoked the last of his tobacco. "It was a real blow for me," he wrote, sixteen years later. "My pipe had been a great solace. I laid down my pipe and, since that day, I have not touched tobacco." He had only half a bag of biscuits and some tea and coffee left. Soon enough, the biscuits were gone.

No ship arrived in 1915. Cardno began to experiment with new ways of cooking caribou and seal, his diet for the coming winter. "I had nothing to do but cook and keep myself fit," he wrote. "Every day I walked ten miles across the frozen snow. My nights were passed in reading and playing patience [solitaire]. Never was a man more thankful of a pack of cards." His tea and coffee lasted until March. After that he drank hot water.

In April 1916, Jimmy Law arrived with news. A ship, the *Albert,* had put in at a post outside Cumberland Sound the previous summer, and left newspapers for the Inuit to take to Blacklead Island. From the papers, Law and Cardno realized that Europe was at war. From Law, Cardno also learned that their employer, Kinnes, had sent a ship in 1915. It was the *Tilly,* under seventy-three-year-old Captain William Stephen. But high winds had blown the ship past Blacklead Island; she was wrecked on the rocks and the captain drowned. The shipwrecked crew had passed the winter at Blacklead. Cardno, isolated only forty miles away, had known none of this.

In the summer of 1916, the *Erme,* owned by a competitor, arrived in the gulf and rescued the shipwrecked sailors, but she carried orders from Dundee for Cardno and Law; they were to remain at their posts until another ship arrived for them. They obeyed, but again, no ship arrived. "Each day I went to the lookout post on the hill and scanned the horizon for a sail," Cardno wrote. "Sometimes I walked several miles to a point where I could see a good way down towards the mouth of the gulf. As the summer slipped by, my hopes faded. Could Germany have won the war? If they had, what had happened to my family, and what would become of me?"

In August 1917, Cardno was in his station house reading a book when Kudloo, one of the station workers, entered, smiling broadly. "A ship, Davidie," he said calmly. "A ship." Cardno rushed outside. A three-masted schooner, *Mary Smethurst*, was making for Kekerten. She had already been to Blacklead and picked up Jimmy Law. By August 28, stores and coal for the station had been landed and Cardno's cargo of skins stowed aboard. On that day, David Cardno saw Kekerten for the last time. "Though my prayers for home had been answered, I left the place with sorrow in my heart," he wrote. "So much of my life had been spent in the lonely wastes of Baffin Land that I could not help but form some kind of attachment to the place and its people."

Cardno made his way home from the northern tip of Scotland to Peterhead by train. His wife met him at the station. She barely recognized him. "Is that my man?" she asked. "Davie, is that you?" Cardno was a slim shadow of the thickly built man who had left Peterhead three years before. But he was home.

The Toll
of the Arctic

I n 1907, the *Dundee Courier* published an article unlike others
that had previously reported on the whaling industry. Entitled "Toll of the Arctic," it dealt with the tragedies that
whaling ships, especially from the port of Dundee, had faced, the
loss of vessels and of life. After praising the hardiness and heroism
of whalemen, it compared their unsung accomplishments to the
praise heaped on explorers who ventured into the same regions.

> The disaster to the Dundee whaler *Windward* in the icy grips
> of the Far North brings home to us in vivid fashion the per-
> ils and privations run and faced by those who year after year
> hunt the inhospitable shores of Greenland and the treach-
> erous waters of Davis Straits for the great leviathan of the
> Arctic Ocean. What tales of adventure these whalers could
> tell of fights with the Ice King; dodging the huge floes that

threaten every minute to crush to pieces their only home in those far off regions; forcing their way through blizzards that raged for days and nights, shutting out every glimpse of seascape and landscape; of almost superhuman struggles against the ravages of frost in order to ward off the deadly, numbing, paralysing frost-bite!

For it is not merely when disaster overtakes a whaling vessel that danger, acute and imminent and deadly, has to be faced. They are beset with perils, known and unknown, all the while they are chasing the monster of the Arctic for his bone and oil, but it is only when they are defeated by ice and storm that the public learn of the trying experiences of the hardy and adventurous whalers. Arctic expeditions go forth with blare of trumpet to explore icy regions that to the geographer are but a dream. These pioneers return to civilisation acclaimed heroes by the public. Their adventures, their privations, their struggles, and their successes are the theme of public wonder and admiration, while the Dundee whaler pursues his calling season after season just as an ordinary matter of course, and often penetrates, when ice conditions are favourable, into more northerly regions than those reached by expeditions whose primary object was not financial but scientific.[1]

The article was no doubt spurred by the loss of the *Windward*, so fresh in the minds of Dundonians. The author invoked it in his first paragraph, and again in the following passage:

---

[1] Anonymous, "Toll of the Arctic," *Dundee Courier* (October 24, 1907).

In Those Days

How far north the Dundee whalers press when on the track of the "right" or black whale, and how near they approach to the utmost limits of unknown area in those ice-infested regions, is brought home by the wreck of the gallant, stout *Windward*. A few hundred miles more and Captain Cooney and his crew would have been in that area marked "unknown Arctic regions." Unknown Arctic regions! Beyond human knowledge, far from human ken—what a fate awaits the unfortunate whaler, unless for some lucky chance, should his vessel be nipped in the deadly ice-floes of an area which offers no mercy to those who seek to find out its secrets and fail! The Ice King is jealous of his territory. He yields an unwilling welcome to those that would invade his domain, and when he shuts the door behind his visitors they are "in the uninterrupted darkness of the very midnight of the great night." Many a gallant whaling vessel has gone forth from the Tay with flags flying and riggings gay with bunting never to return, her stout ribs crushed to pieces in the unyielding embrace of King Ice, and her crew maimed for life by the shrivelling, numbing frostbite.[2]

The author goes on to remember the heyday of Scottish and English whaling:

Yet for a century and more, undaunted and unflinching, ships have left Dundee "off to the whaling." Records show that since 1790 Dundee whalers have followed in the track of the Frobishers, the Davises, the Hudsons, and the Baffins of

---

[2] Anonymous, "Toll of the Arctic."

that Elizabethan period when the spirit of adventure and exploration fired the nation, and raised the name of Britain to be foremost in the world for deeds of daring on seas known and unknown. Before Parry and the noble Franklin had sought to unravel the mysteries of the North and invade the desolate domain of King Ice, Dundee whalers were crawling along the shores of Greenland eager not to gain name and fame, but to land a harpoon in the tough skin of the cetacean, whose oil supplied the lamps that gave light before coal gas became the popular illuminant, and when the market for the produce of the whale was such that at one time no fewer than 129 ships left Dundee, Peterhead, Aberdeen, Dunbar, Leith, Bo'ness, Montrose, and London, Liverpool, Hull, and other English ports all bound for the North.[3]

The rest of the article is a recitation of specific ships that succumbed to the pressures of Arctic ice.

The most disastrous season was that experienced in 1886, when the *Star,* the *Triune,* the *Resolution,* and the *Jan Mayen* were all lost. That was a never-forgotten year with whalers. Such a storm had never been known. The whale fishing grounds of Davis Straits were raked by the most terrific gales and blizzards, ice floes were driven hither and thither, and the vessels were battered with such fury that their timbers burst, and they had to be abandoned. The sufferings of the crews were intense, and their fate can only be imagined had not the other whaling vessels happened to come on the scene. . . .

---

[3] Anonymous, "Toll of the Arctic."

In Those Days

It was in 1902 that the *Nova Zembla* sailed from the Tay on her last voyage. She encountered a hurricane in Dexterity Ford [*sic*], and when she was forcing her way through the blinding fury of a snowstorm on a night as black as pitch she struck a sunken reef. Huge rents were made in her bottom, water poured in, and the doomed ship was left to her fate. The crew, huddled on the ice with only a tarpauling [*sic*] amongst them to shelter their bodies from the piercing cold, were picked up by the *Diana* and the *Eclipse*. The wreck of the *Vega* in 1903 was perhaps the most thrilling in the annals of modern whaling disasters. In the calm of a Sunday eve, the last day of May, the *Vega* lay in Melville Bay. Nothing betrayed the approach of her impending fate. Without warning the ice closed in on her, and in ten minutes her timbers were forced apart. The crew, some very scantily clad, and without boots and stockings, were stranded 650 miles from the nearest point of civilisation. Fortunately the ship's boats were saved, and after six sleepless days and nights in the rigours of an Arctic storm the shipwrecked sailors reached Upernavik thoroughly exhausted.[4]

Depressing reading, the article ends suddenly. Perhaps the author simply didn't have the heart to go any further, for the reader inevitably has to conclude what the author leaves unsaid—that the Scottish whaling industry, despite the tenacity of its participants, was doomed.

---

[4] Anonymous, "Toll of the Arctic."

Captain George Cleveland

Whaler and Trader

In December 1921, members of the Fifth Thule Expedition—the Danish-Greenlandic ethnographic expedition to northern Canada—began to travel extensively along the western shores of Foxe Basin, having settled comfortably into their quarters on Danish Island.

Early that month, Knud Rasmussen and his companions arrived at the Hudson's Bay Company post in Repulse Bay, where Rasmussen met the manager, an old whaler named George Cleveland. His Inuktitut name—Sakkuartirungniq—means "the harpooner." He had come to the Canadian Arctic first in 1895, in the dying days of the whaling business, after being shanghaied in New Bedford. Therkel Mathiassen and Kaj Birket-Smith, Danish scientists, arrived at Repulse Bay shortly after Rasmussen, and stayed with Cleveland; they were tremendously impressed with the old whaler's knowledge and assistance. The expedition's summary report, written by Mathiassen, says that "in rich measure [he] gave them the benefit of his knowledge of the land and its people."

An account of this meeting by the Danish adventurer and expedition geographer Peter Freuchen adds some colour to the event. He wrote that both scientists were "overcome with joy as they met him. 'He is the most amazing man!' they said. 'He knows everything! He's worth his weight in gold!' They had their notebooks in hand and jotted down every remark he made."

While Freuchen noted that Mathiassen and Birket-Smith were both great scientists and suspicion was not in their souls, he wrote, "Unfortunately I have never been a saint, but I was saved by experience from believing in the old man, and I told them that he was a damned liar, and nothing else. I recognized the stories he told as the same old ones that were always used in the North to impress greenhorns."

Freuchen was right, for Mathiassen had to note that "afterwards his information proved not to be wholly reliable."

Decades later, a Catholic priest, Father Lionel Ducharme, wrote down an amusing account of what he had learned from Rasmussen about his first encounter with Captain Cleveland. Ducharme set the stage for this story by noting that Cleveland came to the mission station at Chesterfield Inlet the following summer and "knowing only a few words of Eskimo, he spoke a marvellous language that nobody understood, however everyone got along with him!"

Ducharme then recounted Rasmussen's earlier meeting with the old whaler:

So Rasmussen arrives with his fellow travellers. What an event! Cleveland is everywhere, giving voluble commands to the Eskimos. He invites Rasmussen and his party to come warm themselves at his house. Some Eskimos come in at the same time. Cleveland spouts words and gestures. Rasmussen asks what language they are speaking whereupon his host answers:

"These Eskimos here on the west coast speak a language that I am the only white man to know and understand. For the success of your project, it is imperative that I accompany you—which I will consent to do, provided I am furnished a generous recompense for losses to be incurred during my absence."

Rasmussen said this fell like a cold shower on him and his companions. They recognized an obstacle to their project so serious as to make them start thinking of their voyage to the south, to Sikuligjuaq in particular, as a waste of money and energy.

However, seizing an opportunity, Rasmussen went out to talk with the Naujarmiut, particularly with Cleveland's right hand man.

"Listen," he said, "I speak like people at home. Do you understand me well?" "Of course," answered the man, then the conversation started—in Eskimo of course. It was a revelation. "But what language does your boss speak?" "I don't know." "But you seem to understand him." "Listen. I'm so used to my boss that I understand his facial expressions and gestures. Me, and the rest of us, we imitate the dogs: we obey...."

In Those Days

Rasmussen was relieved. He decided to follow through on the southern adventure, after having thanked Sakkuartirungniq for his services.[1]

This amusing tale is sad in a way. It shows that Cleveland succeeded in doing what few Qallunaat ever accomplished in the "old days"—he lived intimately with the Inuit for years, often as the only Qallunaaq among them, and yet failed to learn their language, relying instead on a clumsy substitute of words out of context, facial expressions, and gestures.

* * *

George Cleveland and Peter Freuchen passed one Christmas together at Repulse Bay. These two eccentric adventurers provided the ingredients for a good Christmas yarn from the prolific pen of Freuchen.

Captain Cleveland was quite a person and not without merit. He lived there, the only white man, and his word was law over a district larger than many states in the United States.

Cleveland was a great character. When we asked him, during our first meal together, whether he would object to our bringing out a bottle of our famous Danish schnapps, he assured us that we could make ourselves at home in his house as long as we desired. "In fact," he assured us, "liquor is my favourite drink—any kind and any brand."

---

[1] Lionel Ducharme and Knud Rasmussen, "Knud Rasmussen and His Visit to Chesterfield Inlet in 1922," *Eskimo,* (Fall-Winter 1977–78): 6.

He was limited to six bottles a year "for medicinal purposes." But, as he was usually ill the very day after the ship arrived with the year's supply, he almost never had any left over for subsequent illnesses.

Captain Cleveland boasted of his cooking and said that he would prepare a Christmas dinner of eight courses, no more and no less. At two o'clock he would start to work, but to gather physical strength and morale for the ordeal he would first have a drink or two. He gulped them down, and we listened to some of his stories. When it was lunchtime he asked me to prepare it, as he would need all his strength and enthusiasm for the dinner. He was going to cook us a dinner of five courses, no more, no less, just to show us that one of the best cooks in the world lived at Repulse Bay.

But he needed a little drink to fortify himself. And after some moments he said that he was about to prepare us a dinner, a *real* Christmas dinner, of four courses, no more, no less. But surely a man deserved a drink before he commenced work.

He was almost stiff after that, but the three-course dinner he was about to prepare would be better than anything we had ever tasted—especially as he was to serve us caribou roast. First, of course, it would have to thaw out, and while it thawed he would occupy his time with a little drink. Unfortunately he took the drink first, and the caribou meat remained outside in a temperature of forty below.

By this time the rest of us were ravenous. Captain Berthie, who had come up for Christmas, volunteered to cook the dinner himself, but Cleveland vetoed the idea. No, sir, he would cook us a real Northern Christmas dinner. He knew that we did not believe in many courses, nor did he. There would be just one course, but it would be caribou roast like nothing we had ever tasted.

It was rather difficult for him to stand now, but he asked me to help him, and I got him into the kitchen where we discovered, much to our amazement, that the meat had not come in by itself. It was still outside frozen hard as a rock, but Cleveland said, "To hell with it; we'll put it in the oven and let it thaw out while it roasts."

Cleveland proceeded with his incredible yarns, but was interrupted by the odour of something burning. We rushed out and found the kitchen full of smoke. It was, however, only the meat roasting as it thawed.

He and I now proceeded with the meal. Cleveland was actually a fine cook. Quickly he took the meat from the oven and carved away the burnt portions. By now the interior was thawed out and ready to roast.

Finally it was ready, a tender, delicious roast. And now came the time for the great Cleveland specialty—gravy. He poured the juice from the meat into a pot and stirred up a delicious fluid. I know, because I tasted it.[2]

---

[2] Peter Freuchen, *Arctic Adventure* (London & Toronto: William Heinemann Ltd., 1936), 334, 338–39.]

William Duval
Sivutiksaq of Cumberland Sound

Wilhelm Duvel was born in Germany in 1858, the fourth son of Charles and Wilhelmina Duvel. When the boy was two years old, the family emigrated to the New York City area—a not unusual move for Europeans of the time, who saw America as the promised land. Wilhelm and his three older brothers, Ernest, Charles, and Berthold, and a sister, Minnie, born in America, grew up and were educated there. Some of the siblings eventually changed the family surname from the Germanic-sounding Duvel to Duval. This represented the first transformation in Wilhelm's life; changing both first and last name, he became William Duval.

At age twenty-one, he made another momentous decision. He shipped aboard an American vessel bound for the Arctic and arrived in the hotbed of Arctic whaling, Cumberland Sound, in 1879.

A legend grew around the circumstances of Duval's arrival in the Arctic. As a young man, the story goes, he was engaged to be married but wanted a year of adventure before settling down. Shipping north, he passed the winter in the Arctic. On his return to the United States, he learned that his fiancée had married a clergyman in his absence. Despondent, he returned to the Arctic, vowing to remain there.

In fact, Duval's first sojourn in the Arctic lasted four years, a time when he was usually employed as second helmsman aboard the schooner *Lizzie P. Simmonds*. Finally, in 1883, he returned to the United States for a year. But the spell of the Arctic was in his blood, and the following year he returned, this time to a whaling station at Spicer Island in Hudson Strait. The next year, he moved to another station at Cape Haven at the mouth of Frobisher Bay. He then went south for another year, but in 1887 he returned north, and this time the move was permanent.

Duval spent many of his early Arctic years at the famous whaling station of Blacklead Island. Employed at one time or another by most of the companies active in Arctic whaling, he was known to Inuit by the Inuktitut name Sivutiksaq—"the harpooner." Like many of the whalers at Blacklead, Duval took an Inuit woman as his wife. With his first wife, he had at least one child, a son, Killaq. The wife died, and Duval eventually took another wife, Aulaqiaq, with whom he had four more children. Two sons, Qakulluk and Natsiapik, did not reach adulthood. Two daughters, Tauki and Aluki, did. Tauki was childless, but Aluki bore a number of children.

The Duval family lived at many locations in the Arctic—Albert Harbour near Pond Inlet, a winter in Admiralty Inlet, Durban Harbour south of Qikiqtarjuaq (Broughton Island), and two years on Southampton Island. But always they returned to their beloved Cumberland Sound. Many whalers, Scottish and American, black and white, came to live and work in the Canadian Arctic. Most of those who stayed for any length of time took Inuit wives and left behind Inuit children. Only one, William Duval, remained in the Arctic for the rest of his life and did not abandon his family.

Duval's descendants are everywhere in the Baffin region. In Pangnirtung and Iqaluit, the Akpalialuk, Battye, and Duval families count him as their ancestor. In 1903, the Duvals moved to North Baffin; when they returned to Cumberland Sound a few years later, Duval's son, Killaq, remained there. With his wife, Tatiggat, he had a daughter, Uisattiaq, who eventually moved to Resolute Bay, the grandmother of the Palluk family of that hamlet. Killaq and Tatiggat also had a son, Kangualuk, who famously disappeared on the shores of Foxe Basin in the winter of 1942–43. His descendants, the Siakuluk family, live in Hall Beach.

In the 1970s, I met Bertha Krooss, an elderly spinster in New Jersey. She was William Duval's niece, daughter of his sister, Minnie. All Duval's siblings except Minnie had died childless, and Bertha was Minnie's only child. "I am the last of my family," she told me. "I have no relatives anywhere." Imagine her astonishment when I told her that she had dozens of relatives among the Inuit of Baffin Island. She had had no idea that her uncle, whom she had met only twice in the 1920s, had had any children. "He showed up here unexpectedly a few times when I was young, with outlandish tales of living with the Eskimos," she told me. In those days, a visit out of the Arctic meant spending a winter, and he often passed the time by taking his niece to New York City to see the shows at Radio City Music Hall. But interracial marriages were a rarity in America at the time, and he never revealed the secret of his Inuit family.

* * *

In Those Days

It is nothing unusual today for immigrants to Canada who have chosen to live in the Arctic to take out Canadian citizenship. A judge presides over a ceremony and welcomes the proud immigrants to Canada. A news photographer is usually in attendance, and pictures grace the pages of newspapers. But in 1923, when William Duval applied for Canadian citizenship in unusual circumstances in an isolated location, there was no precedent, and the government didn't know how to handle the request.

In 1922, Duval went to the United States for medical attention. In those days, a trip out meant an absence of a year. That winter, the Canadian government contacted him in New Jersey and arranged to hire him as interpreter for a murder trial to be held the following summer in Pond Inlet. At about the same time, the trading company that had employed him for many years sold out to the Hudson's Bay Company, and the HBC agreed to hire Duval on his return.

For some reason, Duval decided, at the age of sixty-five, that he should become a Canadian citizen. Ralph Parsons, the district manager of his soon-to-be employer, drafted a letter that Duval sent to the Canadian Government: "Having resided for 36 years in Cumberland Gulf Section of Baffin Land, I am desirous of becoming a Canadian citizen. Upon making application in Montreal, I was informed that I would have to apply to the nearest Court in the vicinity of my place of residence; this, of course, is impossible, as there are no Courts with the necessary jurisdiction in Baffin Land. I was also informed that even had I filled up the necessary papers, and fulfilled all the requirements my case could not be considered in Montreal until next September."

He pointed out that he was to leave shortly for Pond Inlet and would then be landed at Cumberland Sound. He concluded, "It will therefore be seen that to go through the ordinary routine of becoming a naturalized Canadian Citizen is impossible for a person placed in my position." He enclosed an "Application for a Decision" and sent the letter off to Ottawa.

Thomas Mulvey, Under-Secretary of State, had never received such a request before and was at a loss to know how to respond. He wrote to the Deputy Minister of Justice, describing Duval's case as "a rather unusual application for naturalization." He pointed out that the relevant act was unhelpful in this case: "The Governor in Council may, of course, appoint certain authorities to receive the application for naturalization. It is not stated who they may be or where they may reside . . . there is no provision under which the authorities appointed with respect to applications in the North-West Territories are to deal with the application."

E. L. Newcombe, the very practical Deputy Minister of Justice, took the matter in hand, and by the end of June, shortly before the *C. G .S. Arctic* departed for Pond Inlet, Mulvey wrote to Duval telling him that Mr. John Davidson Craig, an officer of the Department of the Interior and commander of the expedition to Pond Inlet, had been appointed a Commissioner "to receive applications for naturalization by aliens residing in the Franklin District."

On September 6, 1923, the *Arctic* was off Cape Kater on the east coast of Baffin Island, southward bound after the trial at Pond Inlet. On that day, Craig accepted Duval's application. The actual citizenship certificate could only be issued in Ottawa, but Craig's recommendation of Duval was tacit approval.

The *Arctic* detoured into Cumberland Sound to deliver Duval home to his waiting family and to his new career as an outpost manager for the Hudson's Bay Company. The next month, Ottawa issued Certificate of Naturalization #26473 Series A, on the fourth of October. Duval would not receive it for almost a year. This German-born man, a whaler and trader, the progenitor of a large and far-flung Inuit family, was the first resident of the Northwest Territories to become a naturalized Canadian.

William Duval, aka Sivutiksaq—German, American, Canadian, and almost Inuk—died at Usualuk, a camp near Pangnirtung, in 1931, surrounded by his family.

The Burning
of the Easonian

The Last Whaler

T he question is often asked, "What was the last whaling ship working in the Canadian Arctic?" And the answer most often given is: the *Easonian*. But in fact, the question is not easy to answer, for whaling did not just end. Rather, it changed, from a pure pursuit of bowhead whales in which a few ancillary products from the Arctic might be acquired in trade with Inuit, through a period when whalers sought the prized bowhead but also any other animal product that might have a value outside the Arctic—like polar bear skins, live bears for zoos, walrus and narwhal tusks, sealskins and oil, and the skins and oil of beluga whales. Once the stocks of bowhead whales were exhausted, the enterprises became trading businesses, but some continued the quest for beluga whales. The *Easonian*, in her final days, falls

175

into that last category, and so meets the criteria of hunting for whales—albeit beluga—on her final voyage.

The *Easonian* was a schooner of 220 tons, specially built for ice work, belonging to the Cumberland Gulf Trading Company, an enterprise owned by Robert Kinnes of Dundee. He had had a whaling operation in the Repulse Bay area and in Cumberland Sound, and had operated a mica mine near Kimmirut (then called Lake Harbour).

The captain of the vessel was John (Jack) Taylor, who had worked for Kinnes since he was a boy. In fact, he is well-remembered by the Inuit of the area, who gave him the name Irngutaq. It means "grandson"—Taylor had first come out on a whaling ship while still a boy, and the Inuit had thought he was the grandson of the captain, who treated him in a kindly manner. The boy had worked his way up through the whaling hierarchy until he was a captain himself. By 1922, he had commanded a number of ships for Kinnes.

In 1922, the *Easonian* was in search of white, or beluga, whales. She would also collect the produce that the company's agent had purchased in trade over the previous winter, an extremely good year for white foxes. Taylor traded for pelts with the Inuit at Ilungajuq—Bon Accord Harbour, not far from Millet Bay, where he knew he would find whales.

But near the head of the sound, the ship developed engine trouble. The same thing had happened the previous year and, on that occasion, embarrassingly, she had to be towed by the *Baychimo*, a supply ship owned by the Hudson's Bay Company (HBC), a new competitor in the sound. This time Taylor had to wait until a favourable wind allowed him to proceed under sail to the whaling and trading station at Kekerten. He beached the vessel there, intending to take off her propeller, then return to Scotland under sail.

But things did not go according to plan, although there are conflicting reports as to what actually happened. One report is that a fire started as a result of a defective switch in the engine room generator, and that the fuel tanks then burst into flames. But another rival trader, Captain Munn, claimed that when Taylor beached the *Easonian*, she lay over further than expected, causing a small petrol tank to overflow. He suggested that someone carelessly dropped a cigarette butt into the bilge, thereby causing the fire.

My old friend, the late Etooangat Aksayook of Pangnirtung, worked with the ship's whaleboats on its last voyage. He told the writer Dorothy Eber about the fire. "It started in the grease around the engines," he said. "It started just like that! The engines weren't working, but some sort of spark ignited the grease. . . . We got some of the cargo off and the Inuit kept on trying to tow the ship [with whaleboats] until the fire broke out to the outside. She burned right in the harbour facing Kekerten."

What is not in doubt is that the ship was on fire on September 10, and burned to the water line. Inuit at Ilungajuq, forty miles away, saw the smoke, as did the crew of the HBC supply ship *Beothic*, which was making its way through heavy ice en route to Pangnirtung. Ice prevented the *Beothic* from reaching Kekerten, and it looked like the crew of the *Easonian* would face a winter poorly provisioned on the isolated island.

An unforeseen wintering would not have been new to Jack Taylor—he had experienced it before. In fact, it was his liaison with an Inuit woman on that previous occasion that resulted in him having a son, Joanasie, in Cumberland Sound. The boy eventually took the surname Dialla—an Inuit attempt at pronouncing *Taylor*. His descendants, many still bearing that surname, live in Pangnirtung and throughout the Arctic today.

In Those Days

Then, unexpectedly, the little vessel *Albert*, owned by Captain Munn's Arctic Gold Exploration Syndicate, arrived in the sound. She was returning south from Pond Inlet and had detoured into the sound to pick up Munn's trader, who was going out for a year. Munn found the stranded crew at Kekerten and gave them passage to Peterhead. It was, of course, customary to extend the courtesy of passage to shipwrecked competitors; one never knew when one might require the same consideration.

Ice held up their departure for three days, but finally the *Albert* left for Scotland. She reached Peterhead in October.

In late 1922, Kinnes sold his Cumberland Gulf Trading Company to the HBC, which was in the process of building a near-monopoly in the North. The *Easonian* was the last of an era, the last whaling ship to sail from Scotland to the Canadian Arctic, and the last of a number of ships to come to grief in the treacherous waters of Cumberland Sound. Her remains can still be seen today near the shore at Kekerten.

The Loss
of the Albert

I f one were to ask Inuit elders what were the most famous ships of old in the eastern Arctic, the answers would probably be the Hudson's Bay Company supply ship *Nascopie* and the government medical vessel *C. D. Howe*. But a few generations ago, the answer would have been quite different, and it probably would have been a small vessel from Scotland, the *Albert*.

Built in 1889 in England as a hospital ship for the Royal National Mission to Deep Sea Fishermen, and paid for by an anonymous donor—thought to have been Queen Victoria—the *Albert* was a sailing vessel built of oak. On her bows she carried the words "Heal the Sick" and "Preach the Word," and around her wheel was lettered the Biblical injunction "And he saith, Follow me, and I will make you fishers of men." Over the years, she was associated with many of the important names and events in the history of the eastern Arctic.

In Those Days

In 1892, she crossed the Atlantic for the first time, carrying a medical officer, Wilfred Grenfell, who was to become famous for his work as a missionary doctor in Labrador. But after a few years, she was replaced and returned to the North Sea.

In 1902, the Dundee Pond's Bay Company purchased her from the mission, intending to whale and trade in northern Baffin Island. The following year, under the command of the veteran Arctic whaler James Mutch—Jiimi Maatsi, to the Inuit—the *Albert* put in at Cumberland Sound and picked up William Duval and a number of Inuit families, and set sail for the High Arctic. They spent their first winter at Erik Harbour, then moved the vessel to a sheltered location just east of present-day Pond Inlet, which Mutch named Albert Harbour. The vessel remained there until 1907, its crew hunting and trading with the Inuit and sending their products home with other whaling ships.

In 1908, Mutch bought the *Albert* from Mitchell and promptly exchanged her for shares in a new venture, the Peterhead-based Albert Whaling Company Limited. But in 1911, he left to work for a rival company and a new captain was hired, John Murray. In 1912, he took the little vessel to Spitzbergen for whaling early in the season, then to Hudson Bay, where she wintered at Repulse Bay.

In 1914, Captain Henry Toke Munn purchased the ship for his firm, the Arctic Gold Exploration Syndicate, despite its name a fur-trading company. It seems that all the principal people associated with the *Albert* had Inuktitut names, and Munn was no exception. He was Kapitaikuluk—"the dear, little captain." Munn had engines installed in the vessel. The *Albert* was busy under Munn, braving the ice to first establish and then resupply his posts at Button Point and later Southampton Island. The latter post, under Duval, proved unsuccessful, and in 1918, Munn moved Duval and his family back to Cumberland Sound, establishing his last post at Usualuk. In 1919, Munn bought out his rival, Bernier, hoping to establish a trading monopoly in the Arctic. That same year, he abandoned another rival, Robert Janes, in the Arctic, after first informing him that he'd lost his backer in the south. The late Jimmy Etuk once described for me the fight on the deck of the *Albert* that he had witnessed after negotiations for Janes's passage south had failed. Munn instructed his crew to rough Janes up, which they did, tearing the hood off his parka and throwing him overboard to land in his own rowboat.

That summer, Murray hired an Inuit crew member in Cumberland Sound for the voyage farther north. This was the well-known Kanajuq, known to whalers and traders as Mike. He took his young son, Akpalialuk, with him. When the *Albert* left Pond Inlet, Mike and Akpalialuk ended up in Scotland, and spent the winter in Peterhead.

In 1922, in Cumberland Sound, *Albert* rescued the crew of the *Easonian*, after that vessel burned to the waterline at the Kekerten trading station. But that year marked the end of an era for the stalwart little ship. Munn's hoped-for trading monopoly had not worked out as planned. Instead, he sold his interests to the Hudson's Bay Company and retired.

The next year, *Albert* sailed from Peterhead under the flag of the Hudson's Bay Company. Captain John Taylor, who had captained the *Easonian* the previous year, was in command. But the ship never made it to the Arctic. In fact, she never left sight of Scotland. Passing through the Moray Firth, she struck a reef and began to sink. Captain Taylor later admitted that he had had his attention on a golf game being played onshore!

In Those Days

The ship was repaired and sold to the Thomsens, a shipping family in the Faroe Islands, where she was engaged in carrying cargo and fishing. Over four decades later, late on the night of May 26, 1968, she was caught in a storm in Davis Strait about 120 miles southwest of Cape Desolation, Greenland. She lost her propeller and sprang a leak. Her call for help was answered by a Norwegian fishing vessel. With difficulty, a line was passed to her, and all seventeen of the crew were removed safely. The next day, the *Albert* drifted into the ice pack and was lost.

I lived in Padloping Island that year, an isolated Inuit community of thirty-four people just off the shores of Baffin Island, a little to the north of Cape Dyer. I was a newcomer to the North and a neophyte in what would become my passion, Arctic history —had I been a whaler, I would have been called a green hand— nearing the end of my second year in the eastern Arctic. I knew nothing of the *Albert*, the little whaling ship turned trading ship turned fishing vessel that perished that night. But over the years, she came to figure in many of the stories that I heard from Inuit, stories of the declining days of Scottish whaling in the Arctic. She was remembered as a hardy vessel. It would be some years before I learned, with some shock, that this famous little vessel had gone down only a few hundred miles southeast of where I lived.

Acknowledgements

M ost of the stories contained in this volume were originally published in the author's column, Taissumani, in *Nunatsiaq News*. Original titles and publication dates are as follows:

"The Mythical Voyage of the *Octavius*" originally appeared as "The Mythical Voyage of the *Octavius*" and "The Source of the *Octavius* Myth" on September 2 and September 9, 2011.

"William Scoresby Junior: Whaler Extraordinaire" originally appeared as "William Scoresby Jr. (1789-1857)" on April 1, 2011.

"Fire from Ice" originally appeared as "Fire From Ice" on April 8, 2011.

"Baffin Fair" originally appeared as "The Baffin Fair" on February 10, 2018.

"The Loss of the *William Torr*" originally appeared as "The Loss of the *William Torr*" on September 23, 2011.

In Those Days

"The Landmark Rock at Durban Harbour" originally appeared as "The Rock at Durban Harbour, Part 1" and "The Rock at Durban Harbour, Part 2" on March 29 and April 5, 2013.

"Inuluapik and Penny Discover Cumberland Sound" originally appeared as "Inuluapik and Penny Search for Cumberland Sound" and "Inuluapik and Penny Re-Discover Cumberland Sound" on July 22 and July 29, 2005.

"A Whaling Captain, a Discovery Ship, and the White House Desk" originally appeared as "The Ship *Resolute* Presented to Queen Victoria" on December 16, 2005.

The first part of "The *Diana*, a Charnel House of Dead and Dying Men" originally appeared as "The End of an Ordeal" on April 1, 2005. The second part is new material.

"May Day on a Whaler" originally appeared as "May Day on a Whaler" on November 25, 2011.

"Words from the Whalers" is a collection of seven articles that originally appeared as follows:

"Borrowed Words" appeared as "Borrowed Words" on February 6, 2009.

"Husky: The Evolution of a Term for Inuit" appeared as "The Evolution of a Word—Husky" on September 28, 2007.

"Yakkie: A Scottish Word for Inuit" appeared as "Whaler Words—Yakkie" on February 13, 2009.

"Cooney: A Whaler Word for Woman and Wife" appeared as "Whaler Words—Cooney" on October 1, 2010.

"Portagee: The Inuktitut Word for Black Person" appeared as "Portagee—The Inuktitut Word for Black Person" on February 13, 2013.

"Sivataaqvik: Biscuit Day" appeared as "Sivataaqvik—Biscuit Day" on July 20, 2007.

"The Mysterious Iisilantimiut" appeared as "The Mysterious Iisilantimiut" on December 5, 2008.

"Guests of the Whalers: Inuit in New England" is a collection of three articles that originally appeared as follows:

"Jeannie and Abbott: Inuit Visitors in America" appeared as "Jeannie and Abbott—Early Photographs of Inuit" and "The Reappearance of Abbott" on March 1 and March 15, 2013.

"Inuit Graves in Groton, Connecticut" appeared as "Inuit Graves in Groton, Connecticut" on March 8, 2013.

"A Reunion: Ipiirvik and Italoo Enoch" appeared as "A Reunion—Joe Ebierbing and Italoo Enoch" on June 20, 2008.

"A Literary Icon in the Arctic: Arthur Conan Doyle" originally appeared as "Arthur Conan Doyle and the Arctic (Part 1)" and "Arthur Conan Doyle and the Arctic (Part 2)" on September 19 and September 26, 2008.

"The *Windward*: A Sturdy Arctic Ship" is a collection of three articles that originally appeared as follows:

"A Whaling Ship in the Service of Explorers" appeared as "The *Windward*, a Sturdy Arctic Ship" on May 25, 2012.

"The Wreck of the *Windward*" appeared as "The Loss of the *Windward*" on June 8, 2012.

"A Bittersweet Rescue and Homecoming" appeared as "The Rescue of the *Windward*'s Crew" on June 15, 2012.

"James Mutch: An Arctic Whaleman" is a collection of five articles that originally appeared as follows:

"Mutch, the Legendary Whaler" appeared as "James Mutch—Arctic Whaler" on March 5, 2010.

"The Whaler and the Anthropologist" appeared as "The Whaler and the Anthropologist" on April 2, 2010.

In Those Days

"Trading at Pond's Bay" appeared as "James Mutch at Pond's Bay" and "James Mutch—Trading at Pond's Bay" on March 12 and March 19, 2010.

"An Aging Whaler" appeared as "James Mutch—The Rest of the Story" on March 26, 2010.

"James Mutch on the Map" appeared as "James Mutch on the Map" on April 9, 2010.

"George Comer: The White Shaman" originally appeared as "George Comer, the white shaman" and "George Comer and Nivissannaq" on May 26 and June 2, 2018.

"Saved by Inuit, Rescued by Whalers" is a collection of three articles that originally appeared as follows:

"Shipwreck at Blacklead Island" appeared as "Shipwreck at Blacklead" on June 3, 2011.

"An Uncomfortable Winter at Blacklead Island" appeared as "An Uncomfortable Winter at Blacklead Island" on June 10, 2011.

"Rescue, and a Queen's Generosity" appeared as "Rescue, and a Queen's Generosity" on June 17, 2011.

"The Murrays of Peterhead: A Whaling Family" originally appeared as "The Murrays of Peterhead: A Whaling Family (Part1)" and "The Murrays of Peterhead: A Whaling Family (Part2)" on March 3 and March 10, 2018.

"The Dead Horse Song" originally appeared as "The Dead Horse Song" on February 1, 2008.

"David Cardno: At Home in Cumberland Sound" is a collection of four articles that originally appeared as follows:

"Stowaway" appeared as "Stowaway" on January 2, 2009.

"A Boy's Life in Cumberland Sound" appeared as "A Boy's Life in Cumberland Sound" on January 9, 2009.

Collected Writings on Arctic History

"Trading at Kekerten and Blacklead" appeared as "David Cardno at Kekerten and Blacklead" on January 16, 2009.

"Exile at Kekerten" appeared as "David Cardno—Exile at Kekerten" on January 23, 2009.

"Captain George Cleveland: Whaler and Trader" originally appeared as "Captain Cleveland's Marvellous Language" and "Captain Cleveland's Christmas" on March 4, 2011, and December 21, 2007.

"William Duval: Sivutiksaq of Cumberland Sound" originally appeared as "Sivutiksaq—William Duval" and "An Old Arctic Hand Becomes a New Canadian" on April 12, 2013, and September 2, 2005.

"The Loss of the *Albert*" originally appeared as "The *Albert* Lost off Greenland" on May 20, 2005.

The following pieces are new material and have not (to date) appeared in *Nunatsiaq News*: "Encounters with Inuit," "The Disastrous Season of 1835," "Over-Wintering: The First Winter in Cumberland Sound," "The Toll of the Arctic," and "The Burning of the *Easonian*: The Last Whaler."

I wish to note a few books that I consider indispensable to a study of Arctic whaling, especially in eastern Canadian waters:

Eber, Dorothy Harley. *When the Whalers Were Up North: Inuit Memories from the Eastern Arctic.* Montreal & Kingston: McGill-Queen's University Press, 1989.

Lubbock, Basil. *The Arctic Whalers.* Glasgow: Brown, Son & Ferguson, 1937. Reprinted 1978.

In Those Days

Ross, W. Gillies. *Arctic Whalers, Icy Seas: Narratives of the Davis Strait Whale Fishery.* Toronto: Irwin Publishing, 1985.

Ross, W. Gillies, ed. *An Arctic Whaling Diary: The Journal of Captain George Comer in Hudson Bay 1903–1905.* Toronto: University of Toronto Press, 1984.

Stevenson, Marc G. *Inuit, Whalers, and Cultural Persistence.* Toronto: Oxford University Press, 1997.

Sutherland, Gavin, ed. *A Whaler's Tale: The Memoirs of David Hawthorn Cardno of Peterhead.* Aberdeen: Aberdeenshire Council, 1996.